CW01023961

# masterChef
## AUSTRALIA

## THE
# COOKBOOK
### VOLUME
### ONE

EBURY
PRESS

An Ebury Press book
Published by Random House Australia Pty Ltd
Level 3, 100 Pacific Highway, North Sydney NSW 2060
www.randomhouse.com.au

First published by Ebury Press in 2009

Text and food photography copyright © Random House 2009
Recipes copyright © FremantleMedia/individual contributors 2009

The moral right of the authors has been asserted.

All rights reserved. No part of this book may be reproduced or transmitted by any person or entity, including internet search engines or retailers, in any form or by any means, electronic or mechanical, including photocopying (except under the statutory exceptions provisions of the Australian *Copyright Act 1968*), recording, scanning or by any information storage and retrieval system without the prior written permission of Random House Australia.

Addresses for companies within the Random House Group can be found at
www.randomhouse.com.au/offices.


National Library of Australia
Cataloguing-in-Publication Entry

Masterchef Australia: the cookbook. Volume 1.
ISBN 978 1 74166 949 7 (pbk).

Masterchef (Television program)
Cookery – Australia.


641.5


Cover design by FremantleMedia Australia Pty Ltd
Internal design by Ingo Voss, VossDesign
Printed and bound by 1010 Printing International Co. Ltd. Printed in China.

MasterChef Australia © 2009 FremantleMedia Australia Pty Ltd Australia. Licensed by FremantleMedia Licensing Worldwide. All rights reserved.

MasterChef™ is produced by FremantleMedia Australia Pty Ltd for Network Ten based on the format owned by Reveille LLC dba ShineReveille.

MasterChef™ and the respective MasterChef logos are trade marks of FremantleMedia Australia Pty Ltd as agent for Reveille LLC dba ShineReveille.

www.masterchef.com.au

Random House Australia uses papers that are natural, renewable and recyclable products and made from wood grown in sustainable forests. The logging and manufacturing processes are expected to conform to the environmental regulations of the country of origin.

10 9 8 7 6 5 4 3 2 1

# Contents

# Foreword

by Julie Goodwin, Australia's first MasterChef

I don't think anyone involved with MasterChef knew what it would mean in our personal lives, or what popularity it would gain with the viewing public during its time on air.

What seemed to the contestants to be a simple cooking competition became a tremendous challenge to be faced. What seemed to the creators to be a reality TV show gained unexpected momentum and became a television juggernaut.

It saw homewares stores sell out of equipment, supermarkets sell out of ingredients, cooking schools sell out of places and people everywhere talking about food and returning in droves to their kitchens.

Standing before the judges at the first audition was one of the most confronting things I have ever done. Cooking, for me, has always been done in the privacy of my kitchen, with the luxury of time to fiddle and fix and taste and try again. I have never liked anyone to try my cooking before the food is ready, any more than I would enjoy people seeing my outfit before I have all my clothes on! So you can imagine how exposed I felt, cooking food with such limited time and resources, for three strangers who, as it turned out, held my future in their hands.

The months that followed contained some of the most stressful, intense, funny, exhilarating and bizarre moments of my life. From the crushing humiliation of a dish gone wrong, to the weirdness of racing through a foreign country with a pig in a bag, to those defining moments when the pastry puffs perfectly, the pudding turns out of the mould, the chocolate cracks – it was all a part of the story.

We met and learned from chefs of an incredible calibre. We challenged them at their own recipes, played their game. We watched and learned from Gary and George at our most valued weekly masterclass. Their creativity, their willingness to coach and to share their cooking secrets, brought us all forward in leaps and bounds. We cooked in pressure tests from recipes devised by some of the most diabolical minds in the food industry. We drew on old family favourites, we relied on instinct and experience, we made stuff up on the spot. We took risks.

We listened and drew inspiration daily from the three men who tasted, reflected, and passed judgement on our offerings. We strived constantly to reach the standard they set and gain the coveted knock on the table from Matt, the heartfelt 'well done' from George or the thumbs up and

# Foreword

MasterChef winner Julie Goodwin's cookbook will be published by Random House Australia in 2010.

cheeky gleam from Gary. We drew comfort from Sarah, who stood beside them with her ever-present compassion and support, especially when the cameras were pointed elsewhere.

We encouraged each other, we cooked together, we talked about food from morning until night. We taught and learned from each other. We shared the experience of being apart from our families, our work and our friends. We lived together in a pressure cooker, so far outside our comfort zones that it felt like being on another planet, but we got through it – part peer support, part dogged stubbornness, part luck.

The recipes in this book are born of the genius of renowned chefs generous enough to share their time and expertise. They are born of the decades of cooking experience clocked up by the contestants. And they are born of sheer bloody panic – faced with a box of random ingredients, what to cook? Faced with a core ingredient and two minutes in a well-stocked pantry, what to create?

What to create? This is the question faced by mums and dads, by chefs and architects, by kids and artists, by business people, composers, gardeners, teachers, human-rights activists, scientists and dreamers.

It was the question faced by the creators of the first MasterChef series. And their answer was to create something positive, something affirming, something that drew families together in front of the television and into conversation with each other. Something that enticed people into the kitchen, back to the magic of cooking, of creating beautiful food from a handful of ingredients. They took a risk – and it paid off.

My hope is that this book continues to fuel that desire, that it encourages people to visit their butcher and their local grocer, to get into the kitchen, to try the recipes, to change them, to have fun with them and to make new recipes from them. To take some risks, to feel the disappointment of failure, which has to be experienced before the joy of success can be fully appreciated. To create something new of their own.

I will always be grateful for my time in the MasterChef kitchen, for the change it has brought to my life and the opportunities it has given me and my family. I wish for everyone the chance to reach out and grab a dream, to experiment and learn and create whatever it is you want – whether it is a great recipe, a brilliant career, a wonderful life. It is all possible.

# Stocking up

What do you cook for dinner when all you've got in the house is a pork chop, half a block of dark chocolate, some flat-leaf parsley, a quarter of a cabbage and a bread roll? While being able to improvise a fabulous meal from whatever ingredients are on hand is an enviable skill and the true test of a resourceful cook, keeping the pantry stocked with basic staples makes the job a lot easier.

# Dry ingredients

A pantry should be cool, well ventilated and not exposed to direct bright light. Once packages are opened, the contents should be transferred to airtight containers. Make sure you label them to avoid any confusion, and try to keep track of how long you have had them. The keeping times given below are a general guide – check the use-by dates on the packet. Don't buy large quantities unless you are using them regularly. Also, try to rotate ingredients by using up the contents of containers before topping up from a new packet.

### Flour – keep for up to 9 months

Plain flour – for pastry, biscuits, sauces, gravy, dusting meat, chicken and fish.
High gluten plain flour (bread flour) – for bread, pizza bases and pasta.
Self-raising flour – for cakes, puddings and other baking.
Cornflour – for sauces, sponges and some desserts.

### Cocoa powder – keep for up to 12 months

Look for dark cocoa (also known as Dutch cocoa), which gives a deep, rich colour to chocolate desserts and baking, and looks great dusted over a finished dessert.

### Sugar and sweeteners – keep indefinitely

Caster sugar – good for use in baking and desserts, as the smaller grains dissolve quickly.
Brown sugar – gives a slightly more caramel flavour and a darker colour to the finished product.
Demerara sugar – has large, golden brown granules, and gives a slightly different colour, flavour and texture.
Golden syrup – has an intense sweetness and mild treacly flavour that work well in baking and desserts.
Honey – can add subtle, complex flavours, rather than just the bland sweetness of sugar. Try to keep it uncontaminated by using only clean utensils to spoon it out. If honey crystallises, sit the jar in hot water.
Icing sugar – good in icings, and where a fine texture is desired, as in some pastry. Also used as a garnish, dusted over a finished dessert or baked product.

### Coconut – keep for up to 12 months

Available desiccated, shredded or flaked. Desiccated coconut is most commonly used in baking. If using coconut as a garnish or topping, lightly toast it in a dry frying pan for a golden colour and nutty flavour.

### Rolled oats – keep for up to 12 months

Used in baking and desserts, as well as porridge and muesli.

### Breadcrumbs – keep for up to 6 months

Dried breadcrumbs can be used to crumb meat, fish and chicken. For real crunch, try Japanese breadcrumbs, called *panko*, which are a coarse crumb, similar in size to fresh breadcrumbs, but dry and crisp.

### Dried fruit – keep for up to 12 months (check individual packages for dates)

Sultanas, raisins, apricots, cranberries, figs, dates . . . there are many types of dried fruit and they often appear in savoury as well as sweet dishes, as they marry particularly well with rich meat and game.

### Nuts and seeds – keeping times vary, check use-by dates

Nuts have a wide variety of uses – from baking to sauces, or just sprinkling over a finished dish. Because of their fat content they are quite perishable and should be purchased in small quantities. Keep in a cool, dark place, or in the fridge if you won't use them up within a couple of months.

### Dried pulses – keep for up to 12 months

Dried lentils, beans, chickpeas and split peas are useful pantry additions, though they usually need to be soaked overnight before cooking.

### Pasta and noodles – keep for up to 2 years

Dried pasta forms the base of a quick meal at any time. Keep a variety of shapes in the cupboard – spaghetti, penne, linguine or ziti – and some lasagne sheets, too. Dried rice-stick noodles, rice vermicelli and mung bean vermicelli are great for Asian dishes, as are rice-paper wrappers and nori sheets for sushi rolls.

### Rice – keep for up to 12 months (brown rice for 9 months)

Basmati – for pilaf, or to accompany Indian curries.
Jasmine – to accompany Asian-style dishes.
Medium grain – for desserts or paella.
Arborio, carnaroli or vialone nano – for risotto.
Sushi rice – for sushi.
Brown rice – for salads, or as an accompaniment.

### Couscous – keep for up to 2 years

Instant couscous is a handy pantry staple which can be used to accompany a curry or flavoursome stew, or as the basis of a more substantial side dish or salad.

### Polenta – keep for up to 12 months

Polenta is a good, filling staple. You can make it and let it set in the fridge, then cut it into pieces and fry or grill it until crisp. Alternatively, a soft polenta can be served with a casserole or stew, like mashed potatoes.

### Dried herbs and spices – whole spices up to 2 years, ground spices and dried herbs up to 9 months

Herbs and spices should be bought in small quantities, as they soon lose their fresh aroma and flavour. For the best result, buy whole spices and grind them yourself. Keep salt and black pepper on hand for grinding and use white pepper for sauces.

# Canned goods

Cans should have no dents, rust or damage, as the seal may be affected and the contents unsafe. Most cans have use-by dates, but as a general rule they should be used within 12 months of purchase. Unused portions of canned goods should be transferred to another container, covered and refrigerated for up to 2 days.

Some canned products are fine, and others should be avoided at all costs! The following products are useful, tasty and make a good stand-by pantry ingredient.

### Tomatoes – check use-by date

Canned tomatoes are great for cooking when fresh tomatoes are out of season. Italian-style diced tomatoes make a quick, easy addition to casseroles, soups and stews, and an excellent base for pasta sauce.

### Tuna and salmon – check use-by date

Canned fish is handy for fishcakes, sandwiches, pasta, salads and pies.

### Beans, chickpeas and brown lentils – check use-by date

The quickest way to use pulses is from a can, as they don't need soaking. Just drain into a sieve and rinse under cold running water. Use them in soups, curries, stews, salads and side dishes.

### Coconut milk and coconut cream – check use-by date

Canned coconut milk and cream are vital ingredients in many South-East Asian dishes.

### Fruit – check use-by date

A lot of fruits aren't available year round, especially short-season fruits such as apricots. Canned fruits are best used in puddings and pies.

# Bottles and jars

Sauces in glass bottles will keep longer than those in plastic. Some products, such as oils, are sold in green or brown glass bottles as the contents will spoil if exposed to the light. These should be kept in a dark corner of the pantry. Most bottles and jars should be refrigerated after opening (check the label if you're not sure), and keep an eye on the use-by date.

### Oil – keep for up to 12 months, depending on the type

Flavourless vegetable oils (such as sunflower or canola) – for deep-frying, or cooking at high temperatures.
Olive oil – imparts a subtle flavour and is good for some simple pan-frying, though it has a low 'smoke point', which means it can burn at high temperatures.
Extra-virgin olive oil – prized for its flavour and colour, and often used in dressings or drizzled over a finished dish. It keeps longer when stored out of direct light.
Peanut oil – commonly used in stir-fries for its flavour and high smoke point.
Sesame oil – added as an 'extra' to impart its distinctive flavour to other oils and in salad dressings and sauces.

### Vinegar – keep for up to 2 years (though a harmless sediment may form in the bottom of the bottle)

Vinegar is used for salad dressings, or to deglaze a pan after frying meat, chicken or fish. A good-quality red-wine vinegar, a white-wine vinegar and balsamic vinegar are always useful in the kitchen. Herbed vinegars are good for salad dressings, while rice vinegar and Chinese black vinegar are called for in many Asian dishes.

### Mustard – keeping times vary (check use-by date and refrigerate after opening)

A Dijon and wholegrain mustard will cover most cooking needs. Use mustard in salad dressing, or add to the pan after deglazing to make a simple sauce. Hot English mustard serves as a delicious condiment with meat.

### Asian sauces – keeping times vary (check use-by dates and refrigeration requirements)

Different Asian cuisines call for their own particular sauces and condiments. The many varieties of soy sauce and fish sauce are invaluable for marinades, soups and stir-fries, along with condiments such as kecap manis, hoisin and teriyaki. Keep prepared wasabi in the fridge for sushi and sashimi.

# Fridge and freezer

Cheese – keep soft cheese for up to 5 days, cheddar up to 3 weeks, parmesan up to 6 weeks

Cheeses for cooking (as opposed to the gorgeous artisan cheeses you buy for the sheer pleasure of eating them) are easy to keep on hand, and have many uses. A good cheddar, parmesan, fetta or creamy blue can elevate a dish such as a simple omelette to a whole new level. When you've removed a cheese from its packaging, wrap it in waxed paper and keep it in the crisper section of the fridge.

Butter, cream, sour cream – check use-by dates

Dairy products are perishable but will keep in the fridge for a reasonable amount of time. Butter can be frozen.

Eggs – keep for up to 5 weeks, though use as soon as possible

When purchasing eggs, look for the carton with the longest use-by date. The date stamped on the carton is 6 weeks after the eggs were first packed. Store in the fridge in the carton. Choose free-range eggs for the best flavour and colour, and if you can find a source of fresh eggs, all the better!

Pastry – keep for up to 3 months after opening

Nothing matches pastry made from scratch, but at a pinch frozen pastry can come in handy. Shortcrust and puff pastry are available in sheets so you can take what you need and keep the rest frozen. Make sure it is tightly wrapped to prevent freezer burn.

Vegetables – keep for up to 6 months in the freezer

Not a lot of purchased frozen vegetables are great, but peas and spinach are two that are acceptable and useful to have on hand. Make sure opened packages are tightly sealed.

Ice-cream – keep for up to 3 months

A tub of good-quality vanilla ice-cream in the freezer means that dessert is never an issue! Drizzle with some melted dark chocolate, or top with fresh seasonal fruits, chopped nuts or toasted coconut. Serve with a homemade fruit pie, or just on its own.

# Flavour heroes

Keep any or all of these on hand to liven up the simplest meal.

Capers – keep for up to 6 months in the fridge after opening

Pickled or salted, baby or large, capers provide a burst of intense flavour. Rinse salted capers before use.

Olives – keep for up to 2 weeks in the fridge after opening

Green, stuffed, kalamata, Ligurian, Sicilian . . . for best flavour, buy olives that haven't been pitted.

Anchovy fillets in oil – keep for up to one week in the fridge after opening

Drain and chop or mash to dissolve into a sauce or stew.

Semi-dried or sundried tomatoes – keep opened jar in the fridge, and use within 2 weeks

Keep a jar of sundried tomatoes ready in the cupboard to toss through pasta or onto a pizza.

Fresh ginger – keep in the fridge for up to a week

Sliced, chopped or grated ginger adds another layer of flavour to a stir-fry or marinade.

Chillies

Chillies can be used fresh or dried as chilli flakes or chilli powder.

Lemons and limes – keep limes up to a week and lemons up to a fortnight, or refrigerate for a longer life

The juice and finely grated zest of lemons or limes can be used in many dishes, sweet and savoury. To have lemon juice ready at hand, freeze the fresh juice in ice cube trays, then store in a snaplock bag in the freezer.

Herbs – grow them fresh and pick the leaves as you need them

The best way to have fresh herbs on hand is to grow them yourself. Even the teensiest balcony can accommodate a pot or two of your favourite herbs.

Vanilla – pods keep for up to 6 months; vanilla extract keep indefinitely

The divine flavour and fragrance of vanilla will lift any baking or dessert. Use a good vanilla extract when making cakes or baked products. Vanilla pods are great when used where the distinctive tiny seeds can be seen – in sauces, custard or ice-cream.

# Gearing up

You can buy a special multi-spouted tool for pouring the perfect eggnet, but when you can achieve a similar result by snipping the corner off a milk carton, as Poh demonstrated, perhaps you don't really *need* one – unless you make a lot of eggnets, of course. It's easy to go mad in kitchenware shops, surrounded by all those gleaming pots and pans, sharp knives, chunky mortars and pestles and shiny techy-looking gadgets. What do you *really* need, though?

# Gearing up – equipment basics

### Knives

Fancy knife sets in attractive blocks are widely available, but you could spend a fortune and end up only using one or two of them. Better to invest in a couple of good-quality knives and build from there. Look for knives with blades that extend to the end of the handle, embedded or riveted into the handle material. A knife should have a good weight and 'feel' in your hand.

You will need a large chef's knife, wide at the base, with a blade about 20 centimetres long. These knives are versatile, suited to a whole range of jobs, from chopping carrots to carving a chicken.

A paring knife is useful for small jobs, such as peeling and trimming vegetables.

A serrated breadknife is best for cutting bread without squashing it.

You will also need a steel to keep your knives sharp. Do this by running each side of the blade at a slight angle down the steel. Occasionally you will need to have your knives professionally sharpened. You will know it's time to do so when the effects of using the steel don't last long. Ask at a kitchenware shop – they should be able to recommend someone.

### Boards

Chopping boards come in a variety of materials, such as wood, plastic, marble or glass. Marble and glass aren't particularly good for your knives and are more decorative than functional.

Many commercial kitchens use plastic chopping boards these days, often colour coded to prevent cross-contamination. This means using one colour board for meat, another for vegetables, and so on. If you don't want to keep a rainbow of chopping boards on hand, simply remember that cooked food should never be placed on a board that has recently been used to cut raw meat, chicken or fish.

Plastic boards and wooden boards with a coarse grain often end up scored with deep cuts that can harbour bacteria. Ideally, choose wooden boards with a tight grain (preferably end grain), and always be scrupulous about scrubbing boards after use in hot soapy water. Rinse well, wipe dry, and stand in a well-ventilated place to dry completely.

### Pots and pans

A few good-quality saucepans in varying sizes are an excellent start when you're kitting out your kitchen. The number of pans you need will depend on the number of people you regularly cook for. Go for at least a couple of medium-sized saucepans, a small saucepan and a large stockpot for cooking pasta, soups and stews.

A heavy base is essential, as it distributes heat evenly and prevents scorch spots. Stainless steel pans with a copper base were once the pan of choice, but today there are many new materials and non-stick surfaces available. Look for reputable brands and feel for weight.

A steamer add-on is often available with saucepans. This perforated pan sits over a saucepan of water and holds vegetables to be cooked by steaming, a method which preserves colour, shape and nutrients.

Ovenproof frying pans (with a metal rather than plastic handle) are convenient, as food such as meat can be seared in the pan, then placed in the oven, still in the pan, to finish cooking. Just don't forget that the handle will be hot after being in the oven – as even our MasterChef Julie did in a moment of pressure!

A chargrill pan is a heavy, ridged pan which sits over the flame and replicates a barbecue grill. High-end cooktops often have these built in. They contribute a slight smokiness to food, and the grill lines give an attractive look for presentation.

Flameproof casserole dishes transfer easily from cooktop to oven, which makes them convenient, as you can do all the initial browning on the stove and then place it in the oven for long, slow cooking. A good one will be quite heavy and made from enamelled cast iron, which distributes and retains heat extremely well.

If you don't have a flameproof casserole dish, you can brown your meat, onions and any other ingredients in a frying pan, then transfer them to a casserole dish for baking.

## Woks

A wok is necessary if you do a lot of Asian cooking. It can be used for stir-frying, simmering, deep-frying and steaming. There are many different types of woks available now, made from a range of materials. Some have a non-stick surface, and you can even get electric woks, which are handy if you have a small stovetop. Round-bottomed woks work well on gas stoves, though you may like to use a ring under the wok to keep it stable. Flat-bottomed woks are best for electric stoves.

What you choose will depend on your preferences and budget, but a basic steel wok, available from Asian specialty shops and kitchenware shops, is good. These woks are coated to keep them from rusting before being sold, so they need to be prepared and seasoned before use. Scrub with a scouring pad and hot soapy water to remove the protective film. Heat the wok and wipe the interior surface all over with peanut oil (use paper towel and be careful). Repeat with more oil and paper towel until the wok leaves no residue on the paper.

Once seasoned, never wash your wok with detergent. Just use hot water and a brush to clean. Dry thoroughly before storing.

## Measuring

Even the most confident cook will need to measure ingredients at some point – particularly for baking, where precision is important.

A glass or plastic jug with levels clearly marked on the side is used for measuring liquids.

Scales are the most accurate way to measure dry ingredients. Sometimes a recipe will give only cup measurements, in which case a simple set of cup measures, in ¼, ⅓, ½ and 1 cup sizes, comes in handy. Digital kitchen scales give the most accurate weight, usually to the gram.

Measuring spoons come in sets of ¼, ½, 1 teaspoon and 1 tablespoon. In Australia a tablespoon is 20 ml, and a teaspoon is 5 ml. Be aware that in the UK a tablespoon is 15 ml.

## Other tools

Wire rack – used to cool cakes and biscuits, so they don't become soggy on the base.

Rubber spatula – made from flexible rubber or heatproof silicone on a wooden handle, these versatile tools are used for folding, scraping, stirring and lifting.

Wooden spoons – used for stirring, and particularly good on non-stick surfaces. You'll need a couple of different sizes and shapes. Some cooks like to keep one spoon for sweet and another for savoury.

Metal spoons – wide metal spoons are good for skimming. Slotted spoons have holes so you can lift food from water or oil, and wide Chinese-style metal spoons are great for folding and scooping.

Ladles – deep, long-handled spoons for serving soups and stews.

Tongs – handy for turning, or for lifting food from hot oil or water.

Balloon whisk – a bulbous wire whisk used to aerate food, such as eggwhites, or to beat sauces to create an emulsion.

Egg flip – a wide, thin, rigid metal or silicone blade on a long handle. For turning foods such as eggs, pancakes or fish in a frying pan.

Masher – used to mash potatoes and other vegetables.

Pastry brush – for brushing uncooked pastry with glaze, such as milk or beaten egg. Also good for brushing oil or melted butter onto filo pastry.

Piping bags – used to pipe meringue or choux pastry and to decorate cakes and biscuits. Nozzles of various sizes and shapes help you to keep your portions uniform and your presentation neat.

Cutters – metal cutters in varying shapes and sizes are handy when cutting pastry shapes or making biscuits or scones. These can rust, so make sure you dry them thoroughly before storing after use.

## Machinery

Food processor – invaluable for chopping and shredding, making pastry, pasta and pesto, or for pureeing vegetables, soups and sauces.

Blender – can be used to puree, though it tends to aerate mixtures. Great for drinks.

Stick blender – purees soups and sauces in the pan, which saves transferring mixtures from a pan to a food processor and back.

Electric beaters – these can be hand-held beaters, or a free-standing machine. Used for creaming butter and sugar, for whipping cream, beating eggwhites and many other foods.

Spice grinder – can be used in place of a mortar and pestle to grind small amounts of spices or to make pastes.

## Bowls

Stainless steel or glass are best, as plastic tends to be hard to clean properly. Eggwhites are very difficult to beat to a good volume in a plastic bowl – copper is the very best for that job.

## Grating

A box grater with coarse and fine holes is useful. Microplanes come in various degrees of coarseness, and are excellent for grating zest, nutmeg, chocolate and parmesan cheese.

## Cake tins, trays and baking dishes

Cake tins – to start, invest in a couple of basic round tins. Standard sizes are 20 cm and 23 cm. (The diameter is measured across the base.) Cake tins with non-stick finishes are common now, but it is still advisable to grease or line them to prevent sticking.

Springform tins – these cake tins have a spring clasp on the side, allowing you to expand the side and lift it from the base without disturbing the top of the cake. This is good for cakes with decorative toppings baked on, and for cheesecakes and deep pies or tarts.

Small cake tins – muffin, patty cake and friand tins are readily available. If you're not using paper cases, line the bases with small pieces of non-stick baking paper.

Loose bottom flan tins – great for pastry-based tarts or quiches. These flan tins consist of a ring (usually fluted), and a flat base that fits inside it. After cooking, the ring can be slipped off the base for appealing presentation and ease of portioning. To remove the base, carefully slide a large palette knife between the pastry and the metal base to loosen. Gently slide the tart onto a serving plate.

Trays – flat baking trays can be used to bake everything from scones and biscuits to vegetables, nuts, meat, fish and chicken. Because they have no sides, the heat circulates evenly around the food.

Soufflé dishes – round ceramic dishes with straight sides, to help the soufflé rise during cooking. These are available large, or small for individual serves.

Ramekins – usually ceramic, glass or pottery dishes, in single-serve sizes for baked or chilled desserts or savoury dishes.

Baking and casserole dishes – large, deep dishes with a lid to seal in moisture, usually ceramic or made from glass or pottery, and used for cooking casseroles or stews in the oven.

Shallow baking dishes – useful for baked pasta or vegetable dishes such as potato bakes. They can be rectangular, round or oval, and are usually about 6 cm deep. They have a large surface area for creating a delicious brown crust on food.

Roasting pans – usually made of metal, and large enough to accommodate a big piece of meat such as a whole chicken or a leg of lamb, sometimes with vegetables around it (though roast vegetables can be cooked in a separate dish). Being metal, they can be placed over a flame to make gravy from the pan juices while the meat is resting. Roasting pans are also used to cook food in a bain marie; the roasting pan is filled with water, smaller dishes are placed in it, and the whole thing is placed in the oven to cook.

## Strainers

Colander – made from enamel, stainless steel or plastic, these are great for draining pasta, rice or vegetables.

Sieve – wire mesh sieves are used for draining solids from liquid. A 'chinoise' sieve is conical in shape, which allows liquid to run out quickly.

Small sieve – useful for dusting dessert dishes with icing sugar or cocoa powder for presentation.

# Chopping up

'If you can't chop an onion, how do you expect to put food on a plate?' That's what George asked the MasterChef Top Fifty as a truck full of onions backed into the giant warehouse where they awaited their first challenge. Chop, chop! A tap on the shoulder meant a contestant was through to the next round. Those whose knife skills didn't cut it would face elimination. 'It's not just a bag of onions,' George told them. 'It's the rest of your life.' Would your knife skills make the cut?

# Basic knife skills

Using a knife is all about balance. Stand with both feet flat on the ground, square to your chopping board. Grip the handle firmly. Rest the blade against the back of the fingers of your other hand, keeping your fingertips tucked safely away.

Start with a slow, even rhythm. As you practise you will build speed. After a while, you will become very attached to 'your' knife, so much so that any other knife will feel strange in your hand. A knife is a chef's main tool and becomes almost a part of them.

### Slicing
Always keep your fingertips curled back, away from the blade of the knife.

### Chopping
When chopping herbs, use a rocking motion and keep the tip of the knife on the board.

# How to dice an onion

1

To dice an onion, cut it in half, then turn it so the root points to your left and slice towards, but not through, the root. (If you are left-handed, point the onion's root to the right instead.)

2

Slicing parallel to your chopping board, cut towards but not through the root once more, taking care at all times to keep your fingers away from the blade. Start at the base and work up, repeating 2–3 times.

3

Finally, slice vertically again from right to left.

# How to julienne a carrot

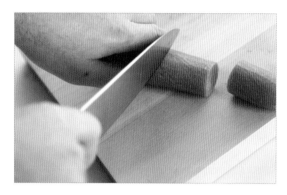

1

To julienne a carrot, first cut it into even lengths, about 3 cm long.

2

Next cut it lengthways into 2 mm slices.

3

Finally, cut each slice lengthways into 2 mm strips.

# How to macedoine a potato

1

To cut a potato macedoine, slice off the rounded edges to square it up.

2

Cut into even 1–2 cm slices.

3

Cut each slice into even 1–2 cm batons.

4

Cut each baton into 1–2 cm cubes.

# Plating up

Whether you're making a wedding cake for someone you've never met with just 24 hours' notice, throwing together a meal for the food critics from *The Sydney Morning Herald* and *The Age*, or just making some toast to eat in front of the TV while you watch a cooking show, presentation is crucial. 'We eat with our eyes,' was a common refrain from the MasterChef judges. So how do you make food *look* delicious?

# We eat with our eyes

The love and passion you put into preparing and cooking a dish should follow through when you are plating it up – whether you are cooking for one, serving the weekday family meal or having a dinner party. We taste with our eyes first, so let the dish shine.

Some restaurant food is like going to the opera – it's a show, it's about wowing the audience, it's imaginative, creative and inspirational. The food is plated like a work of art, with a smear of sauce, a slice of this and a dollop of that. Restaurants use those large, elegant white plates for a reason. They're like a blank canvas. There's no reason you can't achieve the same look at home – but some of your family, friends or guests might privately wonder, 'Where is the rest of my dinner?' The key is finding a balance between the generosity of a homemade meal, cooked with love, and the wow factor of a restaurant dish.

There are no hard-and-fast rules when plating food. It's personal, and everyone has different taste. But professional chefs and food stylists have a few tips and tricks they use to take everyday dishes to the next level, simple ideas you can use when plating up your own culinary creations. Make your food a visual masterpiece, as well as a culinary triumph.

## Style food with height

Body, shape and ooze can make an ordinary dish look mouth-watering. For example, meat and three veg may look more appealing if the four ingredients are stacked in a juicy tower on the plate and drizzled with sauce.

If you have a chunky soup, spoon the ingredients in a mound in the centre of the bowl. Pour liquid in around them so they jump out visually, rising like an island from the sea.

## Garnishes can work miracles

Take a cookbook down off the shelf and look at the pictures. Nearly every main course dish will be garnished with a sprig of parsley, roughly torn basil leaves, chopped coriander or artfully arranged chives. It's because green lifts a dish visually, adding freshness and colour. Finely sliced chillies and spring onions cut on the diagonal are often used for the same reason.

Sauces and oils are also favourites with food stylists for their visual appeal – they make food glisten.

Garnishes do more than make a dish look more exciting, though. They add extra depth, making the flavours come together and completing the meal.

## Make the diner feel special

Individual small portions and little extras make the person you are feeding feel special. In the fishing challenge, the red team served their three-course meal with an extra dish to start – an amuse-bouche of leek soup with crispy Wrasse skin, served in shot glasses. They were bending the rules, but as Matt said: 'Everyone loves a little bit extra when they go out to dinner.'

## Complete the meal at the table

Just serving a dish with an accompanying sauce in a jug and then pouring it over at the table gives a meal a personal touch. Flambéing a pudding or dessert has the same effect. Though they may not recognise it, your guests will feel they have been part of something, that you have somehow included them in the making of the dish.

## Let the food speak for itself

Sometimes a dish just is what it is, and the best garnish is no garnish at all. Think of the tradition of Mediterranean food, in which the hero ingredient is often presented on its own. You may be served a piece of meat on a plate, perhaps with a wedge of lemon. It's the beauty of the food that makes a dish like this appealing. No need for stacking or smearing!

# Basics

Starting from scratch: stocks, sauces and homemade pasta

# Vegetable stock

Makes 2.5 litres
Preparation time: 15 mins
Cooking time: 1 hour

1 onion, chopped
2 leeks (white part only),
  chopped
4 carrots, chopped
4 sticks celery, chopped
1 bouquet garni
10 black peppercorns
12 cups (3 litres) water

Method

1   Bring all the ingredients to a simmer (not boil) in a stock pot, then adjust the heat and simmer, uncovered, for 1 hour.

2   Cool slightly. Strain.

3   Refrigerate or freeze in portion sizes.

Note If you like, roast the vegetables until slightly caramelised before making the stock. This will give it a deeper flavour.

# Chicken stock

Makes 2.5 litres
Preparation time: 15 mins
Cooking time: 2 hours

2 kg chicken carcass and bones
  (cooked or raw)
2 onions, chopped
2 carrots, chopped
3 sticks celery, chopped
1 bouquet garni
10 black peppercorns
14 cups (3½ litres) water

Method

1   Bring all the ingredients to a simmer (not boil) in a stock pot, then adjust the heat and simmer, uncovered, for 2 hours. Skim any froth from the surface occasionally as it cooks.

2   Cool slightly. Strain.

3   Refrigerate the stock, uncovered, overnight. Skim off the fat, then refrigerate or freeze in portion sizes.

Note Cooked chicken carcass and bones will give a slightly deeper flavour than raw. It makes good use of the remains of a roast chicken.

# Beef stock

## Method

1. Preheat the oven to 200°C (180°C fan-forced). Spread the bones onto an oven tray and roast for about 30 minutes, until well browned.

2. Bring the beef bones and remaining ingredients to a simmer (not boil) in a stock pot, then adjust the heat and simmer, uncovered, for 3 hours. Skim any froth from the surface occasionally as it cooks.

3. Cool slightly. Strain.

4. Refrigerate the stock, uncovered, overnight. Skim off the fat, then refrigerate or freeze in portion sizes.

Makes about 2 litres
Preparation time: 15 mins
Cooking time: 3½ hours

2 kg beef bones
2 carrots, chopped
2 onions, chopped
3 sticks celery, chopped
2 tomatoes, chopped
1 bouquet garni
10 black peppercorns
14 cups (3½ litres) water

# Seafood stock

## Method

1. Bring all the ingredients to a simmer (not boil) in a stock pot, then adjust the heat and simmer, uncovered, for 30 minutes.

2. Cool slightly. Strain.

3. Refrigerate or freeze in portion sizes.

Note Prawn and lobster heads, tails and shells may be added to the stock, as well as crab shells.

Makes about 1.75 litres
Preparation time: 15 mins
Cooking time: 30 mins

2 kg fish bones, heads and tails
2 sticks celery, chopped
1 onion, chopped
1 leek, chopped
1 carrot, chopped
1 bouquet garni
10 black peppercorns
8 cups (2½ litres) water

# Vinaigrette

Makes ⅓ cup (80 ml)
Preparation time: 5 mins
Cooking time: nil

1 tbs white wine vinegar
1 tsp Dijon mustard
3 tbs olive oil

Method

1 Whisk the vinegar and mustard together in a small bowl.

2 Gradually whisk in the oil.

3 Season with salt and pepper.

Note This basic vinaigrette can be varied in many ways. White wine vinegar can be substituted with red wine, balsamic, raspberry or herb-infused vinegars. For a light, fruity vinaigrette, replace the vinegar with lemon, lime or orange juice.

# Guy Grossi's mayonnaise

Makes 2¼ cups (560 ml)
Preparation time: 10 mins
Cooking time: nil

2 egg yolks
¾ tsp Dijon mustard
25 ml white wine vinegar
2⅔ cups (600 ml) olive oil

Method

1 Whisk the egg yolks, mustard and vinegar in a large bowl.

2 Whisking constantly, slowly drizzle in the oil, at first drop by drop, then a little bit more quickly as the mixture thickens. When all the oil has been added, you should have a thick mixture in which a spoon will stand upright.

3 Season with salt and pepper.

Note To make mayonnaise in the food processor, process the egg yolks, mustard and vinegar until combined. With the motor operating, add the oil in a thin stream (very slowly at first), until thick and creamy.

# Bechamel (white sauce)

## Method

1. Melt the butter in a saucepan over medium heat. When it is foaming, add the flour. Cook, stirring, for 1 minute. This butter and flour mixture is called a roux. It is important to cook the roux, otherwise the sauce may have a 'floury' taste. Reduce the heat to medium low.

2. Add the milk a little at a time, stirring until smooth between each addition. If you leave lumps in the mixture early on, they will be impossible to get rid of once all the milk has been added. Season with salt and pepper.

Makes 1 cup (250 ml)
Preparation time: 5 mins
Cooking time: 5 mins

20 g butter
1 tbs plain flour
1 cup (250 ml) milk

# Manu Feildel's beurre blanc

## Method

1. Combine the eschalots, peppercorns, thyme, bay leaf, wine and vinegar in a small saucepan. Bring to the boil, then reduce the heat and simmer until the liquid is almost evaporated (about 95 per cent reduced).

2. Add the cream and bring to the boil, then reduce the heat to very low. Add the butter a little at a time, whisking continuously, otherwise the mixture will split. Season with salt and pepper. Pour the mixture through a fine sieve into a jug, cover and keep in a warm place until serving time.

Note Another butter-based sauce is beurre noisette, which is simply 'brown butter'. Heat butter in a frying pan. Watch until the butter reaches a golden brown colour, and you should detect a nutty aroma. You can add a squeeze of lemon juice and/or chopped fresh herbs at this stage if you like.

Makes 1 cup (250 ml)
Preparation time: 10 mins
Cooking time: 20 mins

3 eschalots, finely chopped
5 black peppercorns
1 sprig of thyme
1 bay leaf
2/3 cup (160 ml) white wine
1/4 cup (60 ml) white wine vinegar
1/4 cup (60 ml) pouring cream
250 g cold unsalted butter, diced
white pepper

# Bearnaise sauce

Makes ¾ cup (185 ml)
Preparation time: 5 mins
Cooking time: about 10 mins

⅓ cup (80 ml) white wine
  vinegar
2 eschalots, finely chopped
2 tsp finely chopped tarragon
6 peppercorns
2 egg yolks
125 g unsalted butter, melted
  and cooled
white pepper

Method

1  Combine the vinegar, eschalots, tarragon, and peppercorns in a small saucepan and bring to the boil. Reduce the heat to medium-low and simmer until the mixture is reduced by half. Cool and strain into a heatproof bowl.

2  Add the yolks and whisk over a pan of barely simmering water for 3–4 minutes until very light and mousse-like. Remove from the heat. Add the butter a little at a time, whisking between additions until completely combined. Season with salt and pepper. Serve warm.

# Hollandaise sauce

Makes about 1 cup (250 ml)
Preparation time: 5 mins
Cooking time: about 10 mins

3 egg yolks
1 tbs water
125 g butter, melted and cooled
1 tbs lemon juice, or to taste

Method

1  Whisk the egg yolks and water in a heat-proof bowl until pale and frothy. Stand over a pan of barely simmering water and whisk for about 3 minutes, until thickened and mousse-like.

2  Remove from the heat and add the butter a little at a time, whisking between additions until completely combined before adding more. Whisk in the juice. Season with salt and pepper. Serve warm.

Note To make bearnaise or hollandaise in a food processor, process the egg yolks (with the vinegar reduction or water) until creamy, then with the motor operating add the hot melted butter in a thin stream.

# Melissa's pasta dough

Serves 4
Preparation time: 30 mins +
  30 mins resting time
Cooking time: 3 mins or until
  al dente

2 cups (300 g) 00 plain flour
6 egg yolks (or 3 whole eggs)

Melissa says: 'I have only recently started making my dough in a food processor. Prior to this I made it in a bowl and mixed it by hand. (Super-clever people can make a well of flour on the benchtop and throw the eggs in the middle, stirring the liquid in with their hands.) With a food processor it's easier to make the dryish dough come together with no effort. Otherwise you need to have very strong hands to work and knead the dough. You'll also need a pasta maker to roll the dough out when it's done.

'The quantities given here are an indication only, as anyone who has ever worked with dough will already know that the quantity of liquid to flour can vary due to humidity, temperature and how many glasses of wine you have already consumed, et cetera, et cetera.'

## Method

1   To make the pasta dough, place the flour and egg yolks into the food processor and add a pinch of salt. Using the pulse button, process until a dryish dough forms. If the dough does not come together, add water a tiny bit at a time. Turn out onto a lightly floured surface and knead for about 5 minutes until smooth and pliable. Wrap in cling film and rest the dough for 30 minutes.

2   Divide the dough in half. Wrap one half in cling film while you work with the other.

3   Roll out the dough with a rolling pin on a lightly floured surface until 1 cm thick. Run through a pasta machine at the widest setting, to make a smooth rectangle. Lightly flour the dough, and fold into a smaller rectangle. Turn once at a right angle, and run through the pasta machine again. Repeat 6 times, turning at a right angle each time.

4   Continue running the dough through the machine, decreasing the width of the rollers each time (there is no need to fold any more – you are now making a long rectangle). Stop at the penultimate setting. The resulting dough should be thicker than a spring roll wrapper but finer than a sheet of frozen pastry – around 2 mm thick. You can cut out 8 cm rounds for tortellini, or use the attachment on your pasta machine to make linguine or spaghetti.

# Vegetables

Nothing beats fresh seasonal produce

# One potato, two potato . . .

There are so many types of potato available that sometimes it is hard to know which one is best for the job. Here's a guide to some of the most common potatoes you'll find in your local market or greengrocer's.

### Chats
All-purpose. These are small Coliban potatoes. Sometimes incorrectly labelled 'new', because of their size.

### Coliban
All-purpose (but not really great for mash). Commonly labelled 'washed potatoes' in the shops. Almost round in shape with a clean, creamy skin and white flesh. They make good roast potatoes.

### Desiree
All-purpose. An elongated potato with smooth, clean pink skin and yellow flesh.

### King Edward
Floury. A large potato with a round to oval shape. Clean, creamy skin with pink blush patches.

Floury potatoes are high in starch and low in moisture. They are best for mashing, baking, roasting and for chips.

Waxy potatoes are higher in moisture than floury ones and hold their shape when boiled without going mushy. They are great for salads.

All-purpose potatoes sit in the middle of waxy/floury and are suitable for most cooking methods.

New potatoes are fresh, young potatoes. They aren't necessarily small, but usually have a thin, papery skin.

Kipfler
Waxy. A long, tubular potato with 'dirty' brown skin and yellow flesh. Great for salads.

Nicola
All-purpose. A large, flattish potato with clean yellow skin and yellow flesh. Great for salads.

Sebago
All-purpose, but on the floury side and tend to fall apart when boiled. Large oval to round shape with 'dirty' brown skin and white flesh. Commonly labelled 'brushed potatoes'. They make excellent chips.

Spunta
All-purpose. A long, oval shape with 'dirty' skin and cream-coloured flesh.

# Know your onions

There is much contention over the correct naming of shallots and spring onions. Names vary from state to state, in different food magazines and cookbooks and in the shops. Here is a guide to the names used in this book.

### Spring onion
Spring onions look like baby leeks – long and thin, white at the base and green at the top. They are also known as shallots, green shallots, green onions and scallions.

### Bulb spring onion
Bulb spring onions are similar to spring onions, but the white end is bulbous.

### Eschalots
Eschalots are small, brown-skinned bulbs with a mild onion flavour. They look like a cross between a small onion and a large garlic clove. They are also known as shallots or French shallots. Slightly redder skinned bulbs are usually called Asian shallots.

# How to skin a tomato

1

Score a cross into the skin on the base of the tomato.

2

Place into a heat-proof bowl and cover with boiling water. Stand for a couple of minutes until the skin begins to lift. Remove from the water.

3

Cool slightly, then peel away the skin.

4

Cut the top off the tomato and scoop out the seeds with a teaspoon.

# Crispy chips

Serves 4
Preparation time: 10 mins
Cooking time: 15 mins

3 large (about 1 kg) sebago
  potatoes
1.5–2 litres vegetable oil,
  for deep-frying

George told the contestants that the secret of crispy chips is to
prepare your potatoes and then put them in the fridge overnight
so their wet surface will dry out – but who can wait that long?

Method

1   Peel the potatoes, and cut into long chips about 1.5 cm thick.
    Put into a clean tea towel or large piece of paper towel, and rub dry.

2   Half fill a large saucepan with vegetable oil. Heat over medium-high
    heat until a small piece of the potato sizzles when dropped into
    the oil.

3   Line a large oven tray with paper towel. Divide the chips into 2 or 3
    batches, and lower one batch of the chips into the pan. Cook for about
    10 mins, until lightly golden. Lift out with tongs or a large slotted
    spoon and drain on the paper towel. Repeat with remaining batches.

4   When all the chips have been cooked, let cool for about 10 mins
    (or up to 8 hours in the fridge). Reheat the oil and cook the chips
    in batches again, for 7–10 mins each batch, until crisp and golden
    brown. Drain on clean paper towel, and season with salt to taste.
    Serve immediately.

# Classic roast potatoes

If you're going to do a classic roast chicken (see page 84),  you're going to need this recipe for classic roast potatoes – you can't have one without the other.

## Method

1   Preheat the oven to 200°C (180° fan-forced). Peel the potatoes and cut into 5 cm chunks. Place into a large saucepan and cover with water.

2   Bring to the boil, reduce the heat slightly and simmer for 15 mins, until partially cooked (they should be only just tender when pierced with a knife). Drain.

3   Put the oil into a large roasting tin, and place into the oven. Leave for 5 mins, until hot. Quickly add the potatoes, rosemary and garlic to the pan and toss to coat in the hot oil. Roast for 40 mins, then turn and cook a further 30 mins, until golden brown and crisp. Season with salt and serve immediately.

Serves 4
Preparation time: 10 mins
Cooking time: 1 hour 15 mins

1 kg coliban or sebago potatoes
2 tbs olive oil
1 tbs chopped fresh rosemary
1 garlic clove, thinly sliced
sea salt

# Pomme puree (mashed potatoes)

Serves 4
Preparation time: 10 mins
Cooking time: 15 mins

800 g sebago potatoes
50 g butter
⅓ cup (80 ml) milk or cream

Julie made lamb and mash for her audition and earned a hug from Matt – the very first of the competition. Creamy, smooth mash is the ultimate in homey comfort food, but you can disguise it as haute cuisine if you learn to make quenelles. See the picture of Aaron's beef pithivier on page 176 for an example of just how fine-dining mashed potatoes can look.

Method

1   Peel the potatoes and cut into large chunks. Cook in a large saucepan of boiling water for about 15–20 mins, until very tender but not falling apart.

2   Drain the potatoes well and return to the pan. Place over low heat to evaporate off any remaining water. Using a potato masher, mash the potatoes until no lumps remain.

3   Add the butter and milk. Beat with a wooden spoon or fork until fluffy. Season with salt and pepper to taste.

# Vichyssoise

Serves 4
Preparation time: 10 mins
Cooking time: 40 mins

2 tbs olive oil
2 leeks, trimmed and chopped
750 g coliban potatoes
4 cups (1 litre) chicken stock
300 ml cream
chopped chives, to garnish

Gary taught the contestants in a masterclass that a simple vegetable puree makes the basis of a beautiful vegetable soup. This French classic, vichyssoise, is traditionally served cold, but it is equally good hot.

Method

1    Heat oil in a large saucepan. Add leeks. Cook, covered, stirring occasionally, for about 20 mins or until soft.

2    Peel and halve potatoes, then add to the saucepan with the stock. Bring to the boil. Reduce heat and simmer, covered, until potato is tender. Cool slightly.

3    Blend soup, in batches, until smooth. Stir in cream. Season with salt and pepper. Refrigerate until cold. Serve garnished with chopped chives.

# Pumpkin risotto

George says that when you're cooking risotto, don't stir – agitate! You don't want to break up the rice grains and create starch. The risotto should be creamy, not starchy.

Serves 2
Preparation time: 15 mins
Cooking time: 30 mins

## Method

1  Bring the stock to the boil in a medium saucepan with 1 cup (250 ml) water. Reduce heat and simmer, covered, until required.

2  Melt one-third of the butter in a frying pan and cook the onion and garlic over medium heat until translucent. Add the rice, and coat in the butter. Pour the wine in around the edge of the pan.

3  Add the hot stock mixture a little at a time, just enough to cover the rice. Simmer, shaking the pan occasionally, until the stock is absorbed. Keep adding the stock in batches, shaking the rice as it cooks. This will take about 20–25 mins, until all the stock is used and the rice is al dente.

4  Meanwhile, combine the pumpkin and half the remaining butter in a medium saucepan. Cook, covered, over medium-low heat, stirring occasionally, for about 10 mins until very soft. Mash until smooth.

5  Add the remaining butter to the rice, along with the pumpkin puree and the parmesan. Gently fold through until just combined. Spoon onto a serving plate and crumble the fetta over. Sprinkle with the basil leaves and drizzle with olive oil.

4 cups (1 litre) chicken stock
60 g butter
1 small onion, finely chopped
1 garlic clove, crushed
1½ cups (300 g) arborio rice
⅓ cup (80 ml) white wine
200 g piece pumpkin, peeled, seeded and grated
½ cup (40 g) parmesan, finely grated
50 g fetta
basil leaves, to garnish
olive oil, to drizzle

# Brent's Italian vegetables

Brent says: 'Growing up in Mildura, Victoria, with its predominant and proud Italian population, the Italian ethos of sharing and eating with family is the way of eating I identify with most. It is this feeling of generosity that I aim for in my own kitchen. I would love to be known for the excellence and abundance of my table.'

Serves 4
Preparation time: 25 mins
Cooking time: 1 hour

Chargrilled zucchini

8 medium zucchini, topped
  and thinly sliced lengthways
2 tsp white balsamic vinegar,
  to drizzle

Roasted red onions
and capsicums

2 red onions, peeled and
  quartered
2 tbs olive oil
2 red capsicums
1 tsp white balsamic vinegar,
  to drizzle

Roast potatoes with fennel

4 potatoes, peeled and cubed
¼ cup (60 ml) olive oil
1 fennel bulb, topped and
  finely sliced
flat-leaf parsley, to garnish

Method

1   To make the chargrilled zucchini, heat an oiled chargrill pan over high heat. Chargrill the zucchini slices for 2–3 mins on each side, until tender. Transfer to a plate, drizzle with the white balsamic vinegar and season with salt and pepper.

2   To make the roasted red onions and capsicums, preheat the oven to 180°C (160° fan-forced). Place the onions onto an oiled oven tray and drizzle with half the oil. Season with salt and pepper and roast for 15–20 mins, until tender.

3   Place the whole capsicums onto a gas flame to char (or cook under a grill), turning occasionally until the skin is blackened and blistered all over. Place into a bowl and cover it with cling film. Set aside to sweat for 5 mins, then peel away the skin. Remove the seeds and core, and cut the flesh into strips. Drizzle with the vinegar and remaining olive oil. Plate the roasted red onions and top with the capsicums to serve.

4   To make the roast potatoes with fennel, preheat the oven to 200°C (180° fan-forced). Place the potatoes on a roasting tray, drizzle with 2 tbs olive oil and season with salt. Roast for 20–25 mins or until golden, turning occasionally. Plate the potatoes and top with the fennel. Season with salt and pepper and drizzle with remaining olive oil. Serve with zucchini, onions and capsicum. Garnish with parsley.

# Nic's aglio e olio

Serves 4 famished Italians
Preparation time: 10 mins
Cooking time: 10 mins

5 pinches good Australian
  rock salt
300 g spaghetti alla chitarra
⅓ cup (80 ml) extra-virgin olive
  oil (best you can get your
  hands on!)
1 red onion, finely chopped
4 garlic cloves, roughly sliced
300 g pancetta (homemade is
  the best option)
2 long fresh red chillies, finely
  sliced
250 g punnet of cherry
  tomatoes, left whole
½ cup flat-leaf parsley, roughly
  chopped
2 large handfuls of rugula
  (rocket leaves)
freshly ground black pepper
freshly grated parmigiano-
  reggiano, to serve

Nic says: 'I'd like to share the recipe I cooked for the judges at my audition – a simple, rustic, yet delicious traditional Italian dish. Generally all the ingredients required are grown or made in a typical Italian home. This dish is renowned for being prepared and eaten about midnight after a night of partying. It is quick and definitely hits the spot without being too heavy. This recipe is very close to my heart, as my family originates from Sulmona in the Abruzzo region of Italy. The spaghetti used in this dish is known as *pasta alla chitarra*, a reference to the traditional pasta-making implement used in Abruzzo even to this day, which is stringed like a guitar. The dough is made from flour and eggs, made into pasta sheets and placed over the chitarra's fine steel strings. A rolling pin is used to push the pasta through, creating a square-edged spaghetti. So, here goes . . . *Tutti a tavola? Buon appetito!*'

## Method

1   Bring a large saucepan of water to the boil and stir in the rock salt. Add the spaghetti alla chitarra and cook until al dente.

2   Meanwhile, heat half the olive oil in a heavy-based frying pan. Add the onion, garlic, pancetta and chilli, and sauté gently without burning, allowing flavours to infuse into the oil.

3   Add the cherry tomatoes and cook for about 5 mins until they begin to blister but remain firm.

4   Reserve ½ cup (125 ml) of the pasta cooking water, then drain the spaghetti thoroughly.

5   Transfer the spaghetti and reserved water to the frying pan. Add the parsley, rocket leaves and remaining extra-virgin olive oil. Season with freshly ground black pepper and toss quickly over high heat – just enough time to get everybody seated! Serve with a generous amount of parmigiano reggiano.

## MasterTip
A good-quality pasta should take approximately 8–10 mins. Refer to the packet and use the lowest package cooking time, then do a taste test. This is the best way to ensure you don't overcook the pasta.

# Julia's mushroom and vegetable dumplings

Serves 4
Preparation time: 25 mins
Cooking time: 20 mins

## Broth

3 cups (750 ml) chicken stock
1 tbs caster sugar
¼ cup (60 ml) black vinegar
1 tbs light soy sauce
2 cm piece ginger, peeled
  and sliced
10 dried shiitake mushrooms,
  reconstituted

## Dumplings

50 g firm tofu, finely diced
2 stems steamed choy sum,
  finely chopped
1 oyster mushroom, finely
  chopped
1 fresh shiitake mushroom,
  finely chopped
1 tsp fresh ginger, finely diced
16 round wonton wrappers
peanut oil
enoki and sliced wood ear
  mushrooms, to garnish

Julia says: 'This dish was the turning point in the competition for me. Prior to this I had a habit of sending forth dishes that, although pretty damn tasty, looked like train wrecks on the plate. This was the first dish that I was truly proud of; that I conceived and thought through from idea to plating; that I genuinely thought had a chance of being in the top three. I have a confession – I don't eat Chinese food very often. So I decided on what I do eat often (dumplings) and conceived the dish around the flavours and textures I enjoy when eating them – the fried crunch and the steamed slipperiness of the dumpling, the chewiness of the filling, the meatiness of the mushrooms, the heat of the ginger, the tang of black vinegar, and the unctuous sweet/hot/sour/salty chicken broth.'

Method

1   To make the broth, combine all the ingredients in a saucepan. Cover and bring to the boil over medium heat, then reduce the heat and simmer to reduce slightly. Taste often to make sure the balance of flavours is to your liking.

2   To make the dumplings, combine the tofu, choy sum, mushrooms and ginger in a bowl. Season to taste.

3   Place one wonton wrapper on a flat surface and put a heaped teaspoon of the mixture in the middle. Using wet fingertips, moisten the edges of the wrapper. Fold over, expelling all the air, to form a semicircle. Crimp the edges to seal. Repeat with remaining wrappers and filling.

4   Heat a thin layer of oil in a frying pan over a medium heat and lightly fry the base of the dumplings until golden. Slowly and carefully, pour in a cup of the broth and place a tight-fitting lid on the frying pan. Steam the dumplings for 2–3 mins. Place the enoki and wood ear mushrooms in the remaining broth to soften.

5   Arrange the dumplings in serving bowls, pour over a small amount of broth and top with the enoki and wood ear mushrooms.

# Sam's fried tofu with mushroom ginger broth

Sam says: 'When I lifted the lid on my mystery box in Hong Kong to find tofu, I felt my world had come crashing down. My previous experiences with the soy bean curd had not been my most memorable – but now I'm a convert. I learnt that the key to tofu is the support crowd, the flavours you can bring to the dish to lift it. That's what the trip was all about, confronting us with ingredients we were not comfortable with and putting us to the test. Venturing into the Hong Kong Wet Markets, we encountered a world of produce the likes of which we had never seen. From the dried squid and sea snails to the barbecue pork dripping in the open market stalls, all I wanted to do was dive in and cook.

'Now, the dish below was not a winner on the day (which in the end was a blessing in disguise, given that the Hong Kong super challenge was to follow); however, it is a light, tasty dish and very simple to make. It's all about the balance of flavours and textures, something we learnt was a key part of traditional Chinese cuisine. For anyone who has previously shied away from tofu . . . give this dish a whirl.'

## Method

1. Fill a small saucepan two-thirds full with peanut oil and place over a high heat until it reaches 170°C. Fry the tofu in batches for 3–5 mins, or until golden. Drain the tofu on absorbent paper and set aside. Add finely sliced ginger and cook for 30 seconds or until crisp. Drain on absorbent paper.

2. To make the ginger broth, heat peanut oil in a medium saucepan. Add the garlic, ginger, chilli, mushrooms, coriander roots, spring onions, peppercorns and star-anise. Cook, stirring, for 1 min or until fragrant. Add sesame oil, soy sauce, rice wine and water. Bring to the boil over high heat. Reduce the heat to low and simmer for 10 mins.

3. Steam the bok choy in a bamboo steamer over a pan of boiling water for 3 mins, or until just cooked but still with a little bit of bite.

4. Strain the broth through a fine sieve, reserving the mushrooms. Thinly slice the mushrooms and discard remaining solids.

5. To serve, divide tofu, mushrooms and choy sum among serving bowls and pour over the broth. Garnish with coriander leaves and deep-fried shredded ginger.

Serves 2
Preparation time: 20 mins
Cooking time: 30 mins

peanut oil, for deep-frying
350 g packet firm tofu, cut into 3 cm dice
2 cm piece ginger, sliced thinly
2 baby bok choy, quartered
¼ cup fresh coriander leaves

Ginger broth
2 tsp peanut oil, extra
1 garlic clove, thinly sliced
5 cm piece of ginger, thinly sliced
1 red birdseye chilli, whole
4 dried shiitake mushrooms
2 tbs coriander roots, finely sliced
2 spring onions, sliced
6 Sichuan peppercorns
2 star-anise
1 tsp sesame oil
2 tbs soy sauce
¼ cup (60 ml) Chinese rice wine
2 cups (500 ml) water
coriander leaves and deep-fried shredded ginger, to garnish

# Frank Shek's Chinese mushroom stir-fry

Serves 2–3
Preparation time: 15 mins
Cooking time: 10 mins

1 packet (250 g) firm tofu

½ cup tapioca flour

3 cups vegetable or peanut oil,
  for frying

1 king brown mushroom,
  quartered lengthways

50 g oyster mushrooms

50 g shimeji mushrooms

50 g fresh shiitake mushrooms,
  stems removed, thickly sliced

4 baby corns, halved lengthways

80 g snow peas, topped and
  tailed

3 garlic cloves, chopped

1 tbs coriander root, chopped

1 tsp whole white peppercorns,
  roughly ground in a mortar
  and pestle

1 cm piece ginger, peeled and
  sliced

½ cup (125 ml) chicken stock

3 tbs oyster sauce

2 tbs soy sauce

1 tsp caster sugar

1 tsp fermented chilli bean curd

2 spring onions, cut into 4 cm
  lengths

½ tsp sesame oil

30 g enoki mushrooms

30 g black fungus, torn

coriander leaves and finely
  shredded spring onions,
  to garnish

Frank Shek is head chef at China Doll, down by the wharves in Sydney's Woolloomooloo. He visited the MasterChef set after the Chinese mushroom invention test to show the contestants how to make a *real* Chinese mushroom stir-fry.

Method

1   Place the tofu between two pieces of clean cloth, and place a weight on top. Press to remove excess moisture (this prevents the tofu breaking up in the stir-fry), then cut into batons. Toss the tofu in tapioca flour to coat, and shake off the excess.

2   Pour enough oil in a wok to be about 4 cm deep. Fry the tofu in batches over high heat, turning occasionally, until crisp and lightly golden. Remove with a slotted spoon and drain on paper towels. Drain the oil from the wok.

3   Heat 1 tbs oil in the wok, and add the king brown, oyster, shimeji and shiitake mushrooms. Don't move them around too much at first or they will sweat and the mixture will stew. Add a little more oil as the mushrooms absorb it. Cook until just tender and lightly coloured.

4   Add the baby corn and snow peas. Cook for about 30 seconds then add about 2 tbs of water, which will create steam to help cook the vegetables. Cook for another 30 seconds or so, until just tender but still crisp. Transfer to a large bowl.

5   Heat 2 tbs oil in the wok and add the garlic, coriander root, peppercorns and ginger. Cook over medium heat until fragrant. Add the chicken stock, oyster sauce, soy sauce and sugar. Press the fermented bean curd through a sieve and add to the sauce. Return the vegetables to the wok and add the tofu and spring onions. Sprinkle a few drops of sesame oil onto the mixture. Toss to combine, then add the enoki mushrooms and black fungus. Fold through briefly, and spoon onto serving plates. Finish with coriander and shredded spring onions. Serve with steamed jasmine rice.

Note Though precise quantities are given in the ingredients list, you don't have to weigh out your mushrooms. A mixed punnet of Asian mushrooms should do, or use any mushrooms you have on hand.

# Poh's Buddha's delight

Poh says: 'I have myriad potent food memories of growing up around my grand-aunt and her staunch Buddhist values. At certain points in the lunar calendar, she would fast, only eating certain Buddhist vegetarian dishes, and even though I was too young to understand the religious significance of it all, I would love to go on these fasts with her because it made me feel like a grown-up. A lot of these dishes involve making gluten and with it you can create so many interesting mock meats. You should try this dish at least once, as making the gluten is such a fun, tactile experience.'

Method

1   Combine the flour and salt in a large bowl. Make a well in the centre, and pour in 1 cup (250 ml) of warm water. Using your hands, bring the mixture together until it forms a dough.

2   Turn the dough out onto a lightly floured bench. Knead for 6–7 mins or until smooth and elastic. Cover with cling film and set aside for 10 mins.

3   Take a colander and sit it in a large bowl. Place the dough in the colander and fill the bowl with water, so the dough is submerged. Knead and massage the dough to remove all the starchy residue. The water will grow white and milky. Keep changing the water and massaging the dough until the water is less and less milky. When the water remains more or less clear, what's left is the gluten. This is greyish in colour, very elastic and slightly lumpy.

4   Squeeze dough to remove excess liquid and pat dry with a clean tea towel. Roll into a 4–5 cm thick log. Slice into 5 mm thick dumplings.

5   Pour oil into a medium saucepan until one-third full and heat. The oil is hot enough when a test dumpling cooks to golden in around 15 seconds. Deep-fry the dumplings in small batches. Drain on absorbent paper. Add half the ginger to the hot oil and deep-fry for 3–4 seconds, until golden and crispy. Drain on absorbent paper.

6   Heat a wok over high heat until hot. Add a little oil and swirl to coat. Stir-fry the garlic and remaining ginger until it begins to colour. Immediately add the mushrooms and corn and stir-fry till a little caramelised, then add the oyster sauce, fried dumplings and ¼ cup (60 ml) of water, and toss to combine. Place lid on and allow to braise for 3–4 mins.

7   Remove the lid and add the sugar, fish sauce, and another ¼ cup (60 ml) of water. Cook for a further 3–4 mins, or until the dumplings have expanded and absorbed most of the liquid.

8   Spoon the dumplings and vegetable mixture onto a plate and top with the fried ginger.

Serves 2
Preparation time: 20 mins +
   10 mins resting
Cooking time: about 25 mins

3⅓ cups (500 g) plain flour
½ tsp salt
vegetable oil
4 cm piece ginger, julienned
2 garlic cloves, finely chopped
250 g mixed Asian mushrooms, trimmed and sliced
100 g baby corn, halved lengthways
2 tbs oyster sauce
¼ tsp caster sugar
1 tsp fish sauce

# Eggs and cheese

From perfect poached eggs to Pete Evans' pizza

# How to poach eggs like a chef

There's nothing wrong with poaching eggs the traditional way, but if you want them to look spectacular, this is how the professionals do it.

1

Tear a square of cling film. Drizzle with oil, and spread with your fingers to evenly grease. Lay into a small cup or bowl, overhanging the sides. Break the egg into the cling film and pull the plastic up to gather it around the egg.

2

Expel all the air around the egg, and twist the cling film to shape the egg. Tie the plastic, sliding the knot down close to the egg to preserve the shape. Place into a pan of simmering water and poach for 4½–5 mins, until the white has set but the yolk is still runny.

3

Lift from the water and, using scissors, carefully cut the cling film below the knot. Gently peel away the cling film.

# Chris's egg in hell

Serves 1
Preparation time: 10 mins
Cooking time: about 10 mins

1 tbs olive oil
¼ onion, finely chopped
½ garlic clove, minced
2 tomatoes, diced
splash of Tabasco, to taste
1 egg
¼ cup (30 g) grated tasty cheese
2 rashers bacon
1 thick slice of bread, cut into
  strips

Chris says: 'Egg in hell was my first mystery box win and I was pretty chuffed and surprised that the judges picked it. I am not a fan of bacon and eggs and the ideal breakfast for me is sautéed kidneys on toast, so faced with that box, I had to find an alternative, and fast. This dish was all about texture; the crunchy bread and bacon, gooey soft egg and spicy, zingy tomato. Although it is traditionally a breakfast dish, I like to serve it as a snack and I would be happy to have it any time of the day. In fact, in the afternoon, on a verandah with a great view and a tall glass of Indian Pale Ale, would be perfection for me.'

Method

1   Heat olive oil in a frying pan and gently fry onion and garlic until soft. Add diced tomatoes and cook until pulpy. Season with salt and pepper. Stir in as much Tabasco as you dare (the more Tabasco the more hellish).

2   Place the tomato mixture into a small heat-proof dish or cup, crack the egg into the centre and sprinkle the cheese on top. Grill for 2–3 mins or until cheese is golden and egg is slightly set.

3   Fry the bacon until crispy. Using the same frying pan, fry the bread in the bacon fat until crisp. Serve immediately.

# Poh's century egg dumplings in pork congee

Serves 4
Preparation time: 25 mins
Cooking time: 25 mins

**Congee**
1 kg pork bones
1 cup (220 g) short grain rice
white pepper

**Dumplings**
1 century egg
1 salted duck egg
300 g pork mince
1 egg
1 tbs shaoxing rice wine
1 tbs cornflour
½ tsp sugar
1 tsp light soy sauce
white pepper, to taste

2 cm piece of ginger, julienned, chopped spring onions and fried shallots, to garnish

Poh says: 'I wanted to make this dish in the competition simply because it is very traditional Chinese comfort food. It is everything you expect it to be – uber funk and kind of horrifying to look at. There is a myth that these eggs were originally made by soaking the eggs in horse urine, but in truth it's just a mixture of ash, clay, salt, lime and rice straw. In the process of cooking, the strong ammonia and sulfur qualities of the egg become more subdued, and century eggs are delicious with a rice congee. This dish is in fact very easy to find at your local dim sum restaurant and not as controversial in taste as it is on the nose. I challenge you to try it!'

Method

1  Chop century and salted duck eggs coarsely. Reserve a quarter the chopped egg for garnish.

2  To make the congee, place the pork bones, rice and 2 litres of water into a stock pot and bring just to the boil. Reduce the heat and simmer about 20 mins, until the rice is soft and starting to break down. Stir once in a while to make sure the bottom isn't catching.

3  Meanwhile, quarter fill a wok with water and place a bamboo steamer on top. To make the dumplings, combine all the ingredients in a bowl and work mixture with your hands for about 3 mins, until very sticky.

4  Cut out 20 small pieces of cling film. Place 2 heaped tsp of the dumpling mixture in the centre of each piece and gather the cling film around and shape into a sphere. Tie a knot at the end to secure shape. Arrange neatly in the steamer.

5  Steam for about 5–10 mins, until dumplings are cooked through. If unsure, cut one open to have a look.

6  To serve, scoop some congee into a shallow bowl and arrange 5 dumplings on top. Place a few slivers of ginger on top of each dumpling and then garnish with spring onions, fried shallots and reserved egg.

# Martin Boetz's eggnets

Brent says: 'I had just been given a crisp white jacket with lots of buttons down the front and a big black swirly M on it. When I finally commanded my shaking hands to put the last of the big round buttons through the last of the impossibly small holes, I looked up into the mirror and felt overwhelmed. Today I had a chance at a place in the finals. Arriving at the MasterChef kitchen, I met the judges, who laid out the ground rules. The other contestants were quite relaxed; they had a day off and the mood was circus-like. The door opened to loud cheers and the trumpeted announcement that today's kitchen gladiator from the outside world was Martin Boetz, executive chef and owner of Longrain Sydney and Melbourne.

'Martin revealed his signature dish: eggnets with pork, prawn, bean sprouts and cucumber relish. George eloquently stated that the eggnet needed to be "like beautiful La Perla lingerie, light, wispy and sexy . . . but with crunch". Mine turned out like Nana's pants – but it tasted great, due to Martin's fantastic recipe, which is right in front of you now. Don't panic – have a go. And enjoy.'

Serves 4
Preparation time: 1 hour +
  3 hours standing
Cooking time: 40 mins

**Eggnets**
4 eggs, beaten
vegetable oil

**Cucumber relish**
¾ cup (180 ml) rice vinegar
⅔ cup (150 g) caster sugar
1 pickled garlic clove
2 coriander roots, scraped and cleaned
1 Lebanese cucumber, diced
1 red eschalot, peeled and finely sliced
2.5 cm piece ginger, peeled and julienned
1 long red chilli, seeded and julienned
1 small bunch coriander, leaves picked

**Coconut caramel sauce**
2 garlic cloves
3 coriander roots, scraped and cleaned
2.5 cm piece ginger, peeled
5 white peppercorns
1 tsp vegetable oil
100 g palm sugar, shaved
flesh of 1 coconut, finely grated with a zester
1 tsp shrimp paste, roasted and ground
2 tsp dried ground shrimp
2½ tbs fish sauce
2½ tbs water

**Filling**
1 tsp vegetable oil
4 green prawns, peeled, deveined and chopped
100 g lean pork mince
100 g bean sprouts
2 kaffir lime leaves
1 stalk lemongrass, white part only, finely sliced
½ cup coriander leaves
½ cup mint leaves
1 red chilli, seeded and finely sliced
2 tbs peanuts, roasted and crushed
juice of ½ lime, approximately

# Martin Boetz's eggnets

1   To make the eggnets, strain the eggs, then cover and leave in the fridge for about 3 hours to settle. This allows the proteins in the egg to break down, so that it streams when you make the eggnet, rather than clumping together.

2   Heat a little oil in a non-stick frying pan. Dip your fingertips into the beaten egg and drizzle the mixture over the pan in opposite directions to form a crosshatch pattern. (This is a messy process, so cover your stove with foil before you start.) Once the egg sets, carefully lift the net out of the pan and transfer to a plate. Repeat to make 8 eggnets. If making ahead of time, cool, then cover with cling film to stop them from drying out.

3   To make the cucumber relish, boil the vinegar with the sugar, garlic and coriander roots. Strain and cool. Just before serving, toss the remaining ingredients together, then combine with the vinegar mixture. Place into a serving bowl.

4   To make the coconut caramel sauce, pound the garlic, coriander roots, ginger and white peppercorns to a paste in a mortar and pestle. Add the oil to a heavy-based saucepan and fry off the paste until light brown. Add a little more oil if needed (it can be strained off before the sugar is added). Add the palm sugar and stir until it melts, adding a little hot water if necessary. Let the sugar slightly caramelise, then add the coconut, shrimp paste and ground shrimp. Bring the mixture to a simmer, then add the fish sauce and water. Stir well and taste – it should be sweet and salty. Set the sauce aside and cool to room temperature.

5   To make the filling, heat the oil in a wok and stir-fry the prawns until just cooked, then set aside. Stir-fry the pork, breaking up the lumps as it cooks, until just cooked through, and set aside to cool. Combine the filling ingredients and bind with the caramel coconut sauce. Add lime juice and adjust seasoning to taste.

6   To serve, put the eggnets onto serving plates. Put the filling on one side of the eggnet and fold over. Serve with the cucumber relish.

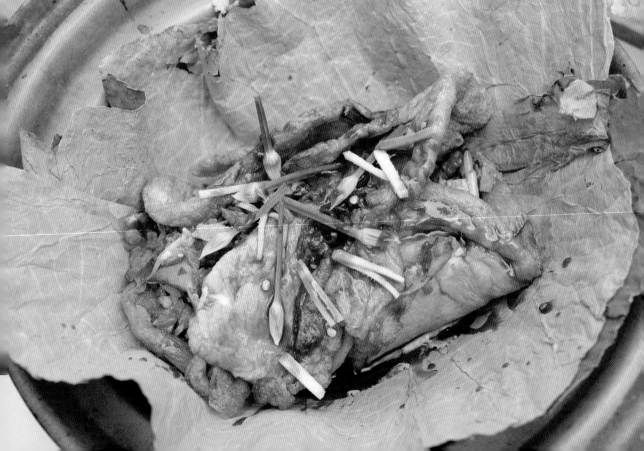

# Chris's double happiness omelette

Chris says: 'The rewards for winning group challenges were immense. We got so much out them. Not only did we enjoy amazing and inspiring meals and meet great chefs, but the time we spent in their kitchens was equally if not more valuable. This dish that I made in Hong Kong was a direct result of winning the fishing group challenge. Thanks to our reward and time spent at China Doll, the second I saw those eggs in the basket in Hong Kong that omelette was cooked! I can't thank the China Doll team enough.

'Make sure you don't over whip the eggs and that the oil is nice and hot. Be careful when you pour it in as the eggs float on the top of the oil and cook in an instant. This dish looks spectacular and has an amazing texture. It is chewy and crunchy on the outside, soft and puffy on the inside and absolutely nothing like a traditional European omelette. You can pretty much fill it with anything that is super-fresh as long as it is light and textural. Do not serve this dish on a lotus leaf of unknown origins or Matt Preston will appear in your kitchen and eat you alive!'

## Method

1   To make the filling, mix all the ingredients together.

2   To make the sauce, stir all the ingredients in a small saucepan over a low heat until combined. Remove from heat. Stand 5 mins. Remove the garlic, ginger and chilli.

3   To make the omelette, heat the oil in a large wok or frying pan. Add the ginger and fry for 5 mins to impart flavour to the oil. Remove and discard the ginger. Pour the eggs onto the hot oil. They should only take a minute each side. Be very careful during this stage as the eggs can easily overcook. Drain on absorbent paper.

4   To assemble, lay the omelette on a plate, spoon in the filling and fold over to enclose. Dress with sauce and garnish with garlic shoots. Serve immediately.

Serves 1
Preparation time: 15 mins
Cooking time: 2 mins

### Filling

50 g bean sprouts
100 g sliced barbecue pork
2 spring onions, chopped
6 garlic shoots, finely sliced, plus extra to garnish
4 shiitake mushrooms, finely sliced
1 tbs soy sauce
¼ tsp sesame oil
½ cup shredded Chinese cabbage
1 small red chilli, finely sliced
2 cm piece ginger, shredded

### Sauce

2 tbs soy sauce
2 tbs sesame oil
1 garlic clove, peeled
3 cm piece ginger
½ small red chilli

### Omelette

2 tbs vegetable oil
3 cm piece ginger, sliced
3 eggs, lightly beaten and seasoned

# Manu Feildel's twice-baked cheese soufflé

Serves 3
Preparation time: 30 mins +
   chilling
Cooking time: 35 mins

melted butter and plain flour,
   for coating moulds
40 g unsalted butter
2 eschalots, finely chopped
2 tsp chopped thyme
¼ cup (35 g) plain flour
1 cup (250 ml) milk
⅓ cup (40 g) grated
   Gruyère cheese
2 eggs, separated
whole nutmeg
⅓ cup (40 g) grated
   Gruyère cheese, extra

Cheese sauce
⅓ cup (80 ml) milk
⅓ cup (40 g) grated
   Gruyère cheese

Hazelnut salad
1 tsp Dijon mustard
1 tbs white wine vinegar
⅓ cup (80 ml) extra-virgin
   olive oil
¼ cup mixed micro-herbs
   (baby mustard cress and
   baby flat-leaf parsley)
¼ cup (45 g) roasted hazelnuts,
   halved

Lucas learnt how to make this soufflé at Manu Feildel's restaurant,
L'etoile, then presented it to his fellow contestants in a masterclass.

Method

1   Preheat oven to 180°C (160° fan-forced). Brush three ovenproof
    dishes with melted butter and dust with flour. Shake out excess flour.

2   Melt 1 tsp butter in a pan over medium heat. Add eschalots and
    thyme. Cook for 4 mins until soft and translucent. Set aside to cool.

3   Melt the remaining butter in a saucepan over medium heat. Add the
    flour and cook, whisking, for 1–2 mins. Remove from the heat and
    add the milk a little at a time, whisking constantly until smooth. Return
    to the heat and cook, stirring with a wooden spoon until smooth. Add
    ⅓ cup (40 g) cheese and stir until melted. Remove from the heat.

4   Combine the eschalot mixture and 1 egg yolk in a small food
    processor and process until smooth. Stir into the cheese sauce with
    the remaining egg yolk. Grate a little nutmeg over the mixture, and
    season with salt and pepper. Transfer to a bowl to cool slightly.

5   Whisk eggwhites with a pinch of salt until soft peaks form. Stir
    one-third into the cheese mixture to loosen it, then carefully fold in
    the remaining two-thirds. Spoon filling into the dishes until two-
    thirds full, then tap them on the bench to remove any air bubbles.
    Place in a roasting pan and pour in enough boiling water to come
    halfway up the sides of the dishes. Bake uncovered for 20–25 mins
    until set. Remove soufflés from water bath and refrigerate until cold.

6   Preheat the oven to 200°C (180° fan-forced) and line a baking tray with
    non-stick baking paper. Turn the soufflés out onto the prepared tray. Top
    each with extra Gruyère cheese and bake for 5–7 mins, until golden.

7   Meanwhile, to make the cheese sauce, combine the milk and cheese in
    a saucepan over medium-low heat. Cook for 3–4 mins, stirring often,
    until the cheese is melted and the sauce is smooth. Season to taste.

8   To make the hazelnut salad, whisk the mustard and vinegar together
    in a bowl until combined. Add the oil gradually, whisking constantly
    until the dressing is emulsified. Season to taste. Combine herbs and
    hazelnuts in a bowl. Spoon over a little dressing, toss to coat.

9   Place the soufflé on a warm plate, spoon over a little warm cheese
    sauce and top with hazelnut salad. Serve with remaining dressing.

# Pete Evans' hot salami pizza with buffalo mozzarella

Julia learnt how to make Pete Evans' famous pizza during her work experience at the Pantry, then taught the other contestants how to make it in a masterclass.

## Method

1. To make the pizza bases, combine the yeast, sugar, salt, water and oil in a bowl, and whisk to combine. Cover and set aside for 10 mins until bubbles start to appear on the surface. Transfer to a large bowl, add the flour and mix with your hands.

2. Turn onto a lightly floured surface and knead the dough until smooth and elastic. Place into a bowl, cover and stand in a warm place for about 20–30 mins, or until the dough doubles in size.

3. Meanwhile, to make the pizza sauce, tip the tomatoes into a frying pan, add the oregano and season with salt and pepper. Bring to the boil, reduce the heat slightly and cook for 10 mins, until the sauce thickens. Set aside to cool, then blend or process until smooth.

4. Place a pizza stone in the oven and preheat it to 250°C (fan-forced) for about 30 mins. (If your oven doesn't have a fan-forced function, just turn it to full heat.)

5. Knock the dough down to expel the air. Divide the dough into four equal portions. Knead one portion on a floured surface until smooth, then roll out to 5 mm thickness. Take the very hot pizza stone out of the oven and lightly flour it. Place the dough on the stone or tray. 'Dock' the dough by pricking all over with a fork, which helps the base to become crisp. Spoon over about 2 tbs of the pizza sauce and then sprinkle with a quarter of the parsley and mozzarella. Top with a quarter of the salami and cherry tomatoes. Cook 6–8 mins or until base is golden and crisp. Repeat with remaining dough and ingredients to make 4 pizzas.

6. Tear the buffalo mozzarella and scatter over the pizzas. Top with mint leaves and serve.

Note If you don't have a pizza stone, cook pizza on a preheated oven tray for 10–12 mins until base is crisp.

Serves 4
Preparation time: 30 mins +
 20–30 mins standing
Cooking time: 6–8 mins

Pizza base (makes 4 bases)
15 g dried yeast
20 g caster sugar
20 g salt
1 cup (250 ml) lukewarm water
1 tbs olive oil
3 cups (450 g) bakers' grade
 plain flour

Pizza sauce
400 g can chopped tomatoes
pinch dried oregano
freshly ground black pepper

Topping
¼ cup finely chopped flat-leaf
 parsley
1⅓ cups (130 g) freshly grated
 mozzarella
200 g thinly sliced hot salami
16 cherry tomatoes, halved
500 g buffalo mozzarella
½ cup large mint leaves

# Poultry

Winging it in the kitchen: chicken, duck, quail and pigeon

# How to joint a chicken

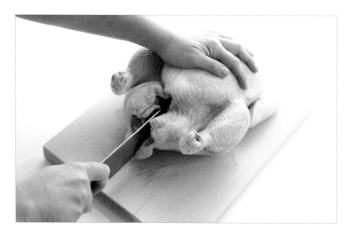

1

Take a very sharp knife or a pair of scissors and cut through the parson's nose.

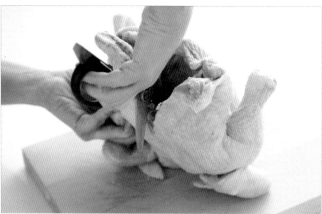

2

Stand the chicken on its end and insert the scissors into the cut you've just made, then cut straight down the chicken's back.

3

Open the chicken out flat, skin side down, and cut through the breast bone.

4

Turn each half over and stretch out the legs and cut them away from the breast.

5

If you need six portions, take the breast portion and cut it in half, removing the wing.

6

If you need eight portions, take the legs and cut through the thin white line running down the middle of the joint.

# How to carve a chicken

1

Using a sharp knife, cut between the leg and the body to remove the thigh and drumstick together.

2

Remove the wing on the same side.

3

Slice the breast meat.

4

If you need two leg portions, cut through the joint between the thigh and the drumstick.

# Classic roast chicken

Serves 6
Preparation time: 5 mins
Cooking time: 1 hour 30 mins

1.5 kg chicken
2 tbs olive oil

A roast chicken is a traditional Australian Sunday dinner. Serve it up with roast potatoes, or mash, or crispy chips – and then make sandwiches from the leftovers on Monday.

Method

1   Preheat oven to 200°C (180° fan-forced).

2   Pat chicken dry with absorbent paper. Place chicken in a large baking dish. Tie legs together with kitchen string.

3   Rub oil all over chicken. Season with salt and pepper.

4   Cook for about 1 hour 15 mins or until juices run clear when a metal skewer is inserted into the thickest part of the thigh near the body.

5   Stand chicken covered, for 10 mins, before carving. Serve with crispy chips, classic roast potatoes or pomme puree.

# Sam's pan-roasted chicken
# with potato and zucchini rosti

Sam says: 'We had barely set foot in the MasterChef kitchen for the very first time when Gary announced with a twinkle in his eye and a smirk from ear to ear that today we would face our first invention test. The "core ingredient" would be a whole chicken. Simple, you might think, but when you find out you have just 45 minutes to cook your bird after a mad dash through the pantry to scramble together 10 ingredients in 60 seconds, it quickly sinks in that this isn't home-cooking anymore.

'I was the last one to present my dish to the judges. After all the dishes that had gone before mine I wasn't expecting much . . . but lo and behold my humble roast chicken was deemed the winner!'

## Method

1   Preheat oven to 180°C (160° fan-forced). Cut chicken into 8 pieces, keeping the skin on. Drizzle with a little olive oil and season with salt and pepper. Heat a large ovenproof frying pan over high heat, add chicken portions and brown on both sides. Add whole garlic bulb to the pan.

2   Place pan in the oven to cook for 10 mins. Add cherry tomatoes and rosemary to pan and cook for a further 10–15 mins or until chicken is cooked through and tomatoes are tender.

3   Squeeze roasted garlic out of its skin. Reserve half. Put the other half in a bowl and add butter and parsley. Season with salt and pepper and mix until evenly combined.

4   Spoon butter mixture onto cling film, roll into a sausage shape about 3 cm in diameter and tie a knot at each end. Place into fridge to chill.

5   Squeeze out excess liquid from the grated potato and zucchini. Place in a bowl with remaining garlic and season with salt and pepper.

6   Heat about 3 mm of oil in a large frying pan over medium heat. Divide potato mixture into four portions and drop portions into the pan. Press them out gently to form flat fritters. Cook for 5–6 mins each side or until golden.

7   To serve, place a fritter on a plate and top with 2 chicken portions and a little rosemary. Top with parsley butter and serve with tomatoes. Delicious!

Serves 4
Preparation time: 20 mins
Cooking time: 40 mins

1 whole free-range chicken
2 tbs olive oil
1 bulb of garlic, halved
16 truss cherry tomatoes, tops left on
1 sprig rosemary
200 g unsalted butter, diced
⅓ cup finely chopped flat-leaf parsley
2 medium desiree potatoes, peeled, grated
2 medium zucchini, trimmed, grated
oil, to shallow-fry

# Poh's chicken rendang with coconut lace pancakes

Poh says: 'I really appreciate this dish as it's a slightly different style of curry than most are accustomed to – it's dry and served with a lace pancake. As with a lot of Malaysian cuisine, the textures here are definitely a point of interest – the flossy, crispy bits of chicken, the richness of the coconut and heat of the spices contrasting with the silky, delicate pancake. I also like this dish because you eat it with your hands, without any utensils, which is a traditional custom of the Indians and Malays. It seems to make the food taste so much yummier!'

Serves 4
Preparation time: 30 mins
Cooking time: about 35 mins

500 g chicken breasts
¾ cup (70 g) desiccated coconut
1 tsp chilli powder
2 tbs ground coriander
1 tbs ground fennel
1 tbs ground cumin
¼ tsp ground turmeric
5 eschalots, or 1 large red onion, roughly chopped

5 garlic cloves, roughly chopped
2 cm piece ginger, finely sliced
2 cm piece galangal
2 stalks lemongrass, finely chopped
1 tbs vegetable oil
400 ml can coconut milk
1 tbs sugar
freshly sliced cucumber and lime wedges, to garnish

Pancakes – makes 12
¾ cup (105 g) plain flour, sifted
1 tsp salt
3 eggs
¾ cup (180 ml) coconut milk
oil, to grease frying pan

# Poh's chicken rendang with coconut lace pancakes

Method

1   Steam or poach chicken breasts. Cool and then shred finely, so the flesh is almost flossy in appearance.

2   Dry fry coconut in a frying pan until golden. Set aside. Dry fry spices until toasted and fragrant. Set aside.

3   Place eschalots, garlic, ginger, galangal and lemongrass in a blender and process to form a fine paste. Heat oil in a frying pan and cook paste over medium heat until fragrant and caramelised.

4   Add chicken, dry spice mixture, coconut milk and sugar to eschalot mixture. Cook until sauce has reduced slightly. Add toasted coconut. This will absorb most of the sauce. Keep cooking till mixture is quite dry and forms a golden crust on the underside, and keep tossing until all the chicken has a crispy, golden appearance.

5   To make the pancakes, whisk flour, salt and eggs in a large jug until completely smooth. Add coconut milk to make the batter the consistency of pouring cream. Pass mixture through a sieve to give a very smooth texture.

6   Heat a lightly oiled non-stick frying pan over medium heat. Make sure the pan is sufficiently hot before attempting a pancake. Pour batter into the empty milk carton (see note), and in a tight zigzag motion pour a thin stream from one side of the pan to the other. Repeat the action at right angles to form a crosshatch pattern. To complete, move in concentric circles around the outer edge of the crosshatching to knit the lattice together and make the pancake stable enough to pick up.

7   Using a butter knife, flick up an edge and gently pick the pancake up with your fingers. Flip onto the other side and cook for 2 seconds. Place the pancake on a plate. Repeat with remaining pancake batter to make 12 pancakes.

8   Serve the pancakes hot or at room temperature with the chicken rendang, freshly sliced cucumber and a wedge of lime.

Note  To make a pouring vessel for the pancake batter, slice a 3 mm diameter corner off a small, clean milk carton. If the hole is too small the mixture will not pass through it smoothly. If too large, the batter will pour too quickly, resulting in thick pancakes, not fine, lace-like ones.

# Kate's traditional Goan chicken curry

Kate says: 'This recipe is very special to me because it was taught to me by my grandmother. My father is from Goa, a Portuguese-influenced region on the south-west coast of India, so I decided to go back to my roots when I cooked this dish for the judges. George found this dish really hot, so if you aren't a chilli fan it's probably not for you. However, a milder curry can be achieved by adding more coconut milk to taste.'

Serves 4
Preparation time: 30 mins
Cooking time: about 1 hour

2 tbs vegetable oil
1 onion, finely diced
3 cm piece of ginger,
  finely grated
5 garlic cloves, crushed
4 tomatoes, finely diced
500 g chicken thigh fillets,
  quartered
400 ml can coconut milk
4 large potatoes, peeled
  and quartered
2 tbs malt vinegar
coriander, to garnish

Masala
3 red Kashmiri chillies
1½ tsp coriander seeds
1 tsp ground cinnamon
¾ tsp cumin seeds
½ tsp whole peppercorns
½ tsp whole cloves
½ tsp ground turmeric

'I've got shivers . . .
this dish is fantastic.' – Matt

Method

1   To make the masala, process all ingredients in a spice grinder or mortar and pestle until finely ground. Set aside.

2   Heat the oil in a large non-stick frying pan over medium-high heat and fry onion, ginger and garlic until lightly browned. Add tomatoes to the pan and fry until they start to break down. It is important to fry the tomato for quite some time as this will form the base of a nice thick gravy for the curry.

3   Add the masala to the pan and fry for 2 mins. The mixture should be very fragrant.

4   Add chicken and coat with the spice mixture. Fry for a couple of mins and then add coconut milk. Bring to the boil, reduce heat to medium low and simmer for 20 mins. Add potatoes. If the mixture is too dry, add some more coconut milk or ½ cup (125 ml) water. Simmer for another 20 mins or until potatoes are tender and chicken is cooked through. Season with vinegar, salt and pepper, then garnish with coriander and serve.

Note Kashmiri chillies are an Indian chilli which give a wonderful red colour to curries. They are available dried through spice specialists (try online).

# Michelle's chicken with preserved lemon

Michelle says: 'Exploring flavours from around the world is a great joy . . . it's like taking my tastebuds on a mini-holiday. In this recipe I have included some of my favourite aromatic flavours, like star-anise, cumin seeds and coriander. Free-range chicken marinated in garlic and preserved lemon with a sweet pomegranate salsa reminds me of balmy nights under a canopy at the casbah! Best wishes, and may you find joy in the journey.'

Serves 4
Preparation time: 20 mins +
  10 mins marinating
Cooking time: 35 mins

2 cups (500 ml) chicken stock
4 star-anise
4 garlic cloves, finely chopped
1 cup (180 g) blanched almonds
2 tsp cumin seeds
3 preserved lemon quarters,
  plus 2 tbs of preserving liquid
4 free-range chicken breasts,
  skin on
⅓ cup olive oil
1 tsp ground coriander
1 bunch bulb spring onions,
  trimmed, halved
1 cup (200 g) couscous
seeds and juice of
  1 pomegranate
200 g yellow or green beans

Method

1  Preheat oven to 180°C (160° fan-forced). Bring stock to the boil in a medium saucepan. Add 3 star-anise and half the garlic. Season to taste. Reduce heat and simmer, uncovered, until reduced to 1¼ cups (310 ml). Strain.

2  Meanwhile, heat a non-stick frying pan over medium heat and dry fry almonds until lightly browned. Transfer to a chopping board, cool and roughly chop. Using the same frying pan, repeat with cumin seeds.

3  Remove and discard pulp from lemon quarters. Finely slice rind and set aside.

4  Place chicken breasts, cumin seeds, 1 tbs of the lemon preserving liquid, 2 tbs oil, coriander and remaining garlic in a bowl. Toss to combine. Refrigerate, covered, to marinate for 10 mins.

5  Heat an ovenproof frying pan over medium heat. Add chicken breasts and spring onions. Cook, turning the chicken until browned on both sides. Place on an oven tray with onions. Cook in the oven a further 15–20 mins, or until cooked through.

6  Reheat the stock until boiling and combine in a bowl with the couscous, 1 tbs of remaining oil, almonds, half the pomegranate seeds and juice. Cover tightly and set aside for 5 mins. Uncover, season and fluff up the grains with a fork.

7  Cook the beans in a small saucepan of boiling water for 2 mins or until tender. Drain, then combine in a bowl with remaining oil, pomegranate seeds and juice, and preserving liquid. Season to taste.

8  To serve, arrange couscous on a plate and top with sliced chicken breast, beans and preserved lemon rind. Drizzle pomegranate mixture around the plate, then add caramelised spring onions.

# Justine's duck with sauce aigre douce

Serves 2
Preparation time: 1 hour
Cooking time: about 40 mins

Justine says: 'One of the proudest moments I had on MasterChef was when I developed this dish and served it to Jacques Reymond, Margaret Fulton, Armando Percuoco and Cheong Liew. This elegant main course dish has great balance between sweet and sour – known as *aigre douce* in French. It also has a real emphasis on seasonality, something I am passionate about. In this case it is a winter dish; however, you can modify it to your liking. For example, you can add olives to the sauce or change the garnish to suit the season, such as a medley of fresh peas, baby zucchini and asparagus in the warmer months.'

2 duck breasts, skin on
2 tbs sugar
¼ cup (60 ml) red wine vinegar
½ cup (125 ml) veal glaze or stock
zest of 1 orange, finely grated
¼ cup (60 ml) orange juice
20 g butter, chopped

Mini eschalot tartes tatin
40 g butter
1 tbs olive oil
6 eschalots, peeled and left
  whole
1 sprig thyme
¼ cup (60 ml) balsamic vinegar
1 tsp caster sugar
1 sheet good-quality puff pastry

Celeriac puree
40 g butter
1 bulb celeriac, peeled and
  chopped
1 bay leaf
½ cup (125 ml) cream
1 cup (250 ml) milk

Carrots
1 tbs olive oil
1 garlic clove, finely chopped
1 bunch of Dutch carrots,
  peeled and trimmed
2 cloves
1 sprig thyme
¼ cup (60 ml) chicken stock
1 tbs cream

# Justine's duck with sauce aigre douce

'I'd like the recipe!'
– Margaret Fulton

'A perfect seasonal dish.'
– Jacques Reymond

Method

1   For the mini eschalot tartes tatin, preheat oven to 180°C (160° fan-forced). Melt butter and oil in a saucepan. Cook eschalots whole over a low heat (this will ensure they do not fall apart too much) for about 5 mins, or until starting to soften. Add thyme, balsamic vinegar and sugar. Cook over a low heat, stirring occasionally, for 20 mins. Cool slightly.

2   Lightly grease 2 holes of a medium muffin tray (⅓ cup capacity). Use a 9 cm round cutter to cut out two circles of puff pastry, slightly larger than the muffin holes. Arrange eschalots over bases of prepared pan holes and drizzle with a couple of teaspoons of balsamic syrup from the pan. Top with the circles of pastry, tucking them in around the sides (like a blanket!). Cook for 15 mins, until the pastry is golden brown. Cool. Remove tartes tatin from the tin with a spatula. Their tops will be dark from the caramelised vinegar and sugar. Leave the oven on.

3   To make the celeriac puree, melt butter in a saucepan. Cook celeriac briefly, ensuring it does not go brown. Add bay leaf, cream and milk. Season with salt. Simmer for 15 mins or until tender. While still hot, but not boiling, blend the mixture until smooth. Push through a sieve for a silkier texture. Cover to keep warm.

4   Meanwhile, for the carrots, heat oil and garlic in a saucepan. Add carrots, cloves, thyme and stock. Simmer covered for 8 mins or until carrots are tender. Stir in cream.

5   Score duck skin deeply with a criss-cross pattern. Season well with salt and pepper. Heat an ovenproof frying pan on high. Add duck breasts, skin-side down. Your aim is to melt the fat and form a crispy golden skin; this should take 3–4 mins. Turn and cook the other side for about 2–3 mins. Transfer to the oven and cook for a further 6–8 mins (depending on the size of your duck breasts). Transfer to a plate and rest in a warm spot for a further 3–4 mins. Slice thickly.

6   For the sauce, sprinkle sugar into the pan that you cooked the duck in. Cook over medium heat until it melts and forms a caramel. Add red wine vinegar. Stir to combine. Add veal glaze and reduce slightly. Add orange zest and juice and reduce again until thick and glossy. Whisk in butter.

7   To serve, smear celeriac puree across serving plate. Top with tarte tatin. Serve with duck, sauce and carrots.

# Pete Evans' tea-smoked duck breast

Serves 2
Preparation time: 45 mins
Cooking time: 20 mins

2 duck breast fillets
3 cups (120 g) baby spinach
  leaves
sea salt
vegetable oil, to deep fry
2 tbs ginger, julienned

Ravioli
50 g pâté
25 g water chestnuts, diced
25 g pear, diced
4 gow gee or won ton wrappers

Tea smoking mixture
½ cup (40 g) oolong tea leaves
½ cup (40 g) jasmine tea leaves
zest of 3 oranges, cut in wide
  strips
4 pieces of dried orange peel
1 cup (225 g) jasmine rice
1 cup (200 g) brown sugar
5 whole star-anise
1 tbs Sichuan peppercorns
6 pieces cassia bark

Orange sauce
1½ tbs caster sugar
1½ tbs red wine vinegar
1 cup (250 ml) blood orange
  juice or orange juice
½ cup (125 ml) Peking duck
  stock or chicken stock
finely grated zest of ½ orange
25 g butter, diced

Julia says: 'My thoughts on seeing this dish were something along the lines of, "Oh my God, that looks complicated. And delicious!". Upon seeing the recipe it changed to, "Okay, so only about ten million ingredients there, then." And once I tasted it? "How on earth am I going to get duck that tender, that flavoursome, and all those elements on the plate?" Having only cooked duck a few times (and most of those times were unmitigated disasters) and never smoked anything before, I was worried, to say the least.

'In this dish, Pete Evans has pulled together convivial flavours and contrasting textures to create a truly beautiful Asian spin on the classic duck à l'orange. Cooking it takes some restraint. Take care not to burn the caramel for the sauce, but don't undercook the sugar either; don't overcook the duck as you smoke it or sear it; be careful to render the duck fat in the pan so you get a nice crisp skin; lightly fry the ravioli to create a slight crispness; and don't overfry the ginger!

'I credit Pete's instruction for me pulling off this dish; he is a gifted teacher and so willing to share his knowledge. Three nines out of ten and a ticket straight through to the finals – it was certainly an unexpected result for all concerned. Thank you, Pete!'

# Pete Evans' tea-smoked duck breast

## Method

1. To smoke the duck, line a wok with foil, then place the combined tea smoking mixture onto the foil. Turn on the heat to medium and wait for the mixture to start to smoke. Once smoking, place duck breasts, skin side down, in the middle tray of a steamer, or on a rack that fits into the wok. Cover with a lid and cook for 7 mins or until rare.

2. To make the orange sauce, place sugar in a cold pan and melt it down slowly, taking care not to burn. Add vinegar and simmer until sugar is dissolved. Add orange juice and bring to the boil. Reduce heat slightly and simmer until reduced by half. Add stock and simmer again until reduced by half. Add orange zest and whisk in butter. Season to taste.

3. To make the ravioli, mix pâté, water chestnuts and pear together with a pinch of salt. Lay 2 gow gee wrappers on the bench and brush with water. Divide pâté mixture between the two wrappers, placing half in the centre of each. Place the other gow gee wrappers over the filling and press down firmly around the edges to seal.

4. Place the duck skin side down in a hot frying pan and cook until fat has rendered (melted) and skin is crispy. Transfer to a warm plate to rest for a few mins and then cut into slices.

5. Add the spinach to the same pan and cook until just wilted. Season with sea salt and pepper, then strain off any excess liquid. Drop ravioli into a pot of boiling water to cook for 1 min.

6. Pour vegetable oil into a small frying pan until a quarter full. Heat over medium-high heat until hot. Deep-fry ginger for 3–4 mins or until golden and crispy. Drain on absorbent paper and sprinkle with a little salt. Set aside. Reheat orange sauce.

7. To serve, place spinach on serving plates. Top with sliced duck and ravioli. Drizzle with sauce and top with fried ginger.

Note Any leftover sauce will keep in the fridge for up to 4 days.

# Sweet and sour duck with ho fun noodles

Serves 1
Preparation time: 20 mins
Cooking time: 3 mins

¼ cup (60 ml) white vinegar
¼ cup (55 g) sugar
120 g young ginger, peeled
  and thinly sliced
80 g ho fun rice noodles
1 duck breast fillet
1 eggwhite
1 tsp cornflour
2 tsp light soy sauce
2 tbs vegetable oil
2 garlic cloves, thinly sliced
1 long red chilli, cut into
  2 cm diamond shapes
1 long green chilli, cut into
  2 cm diamond shapes
150 g fresh peeled pineapple,
  cut into 2 cm dice
2 tsp Chinese rice wine
2 spring onions, white part only,
  cut into 3 cm pieces

Sauce
½ tsp cornflour
¼ cup (60 ml) chicken stock
2 tsp light soy sauce
½ tsp sesame oil
salt and white pepper to season

After the Hong Kong suckling pig super challenge, Justine and Julie faced a pressure test: sweet and sour duck with ho fun noodles. It was Justine's first pressure test and Julie's fourth. Matt told Julie she had survived so many pressure tests she should be called 'the Eliminator' – and sure enough, she made it through again. Justine was the unlucky one who was sent home – but as it turned out, not for long! And no-one was happier than Julie to see her return.

Method

1   Combine vinegar and sugar in a small saucepan. Stir over low heat to dissolve sugar and remove from heat. Wash ginger slices in a bowl of lightly salted water and drain. Add ginger to sugar and vinegar mixture and soak for 15 mins, then drain.

2   Meanwhile, soak noodles in hot water for 2–3 mins, until just soft. Gently separate noodles. Drain.

3   Remove skin from duck and cut flesh into thin slices. Place in a bowl with eggwhite, cornflour and light soy sauce. Set aside.

4   To make the sauce, dissolve the cornflour in 1 tbs stock. Combine cornflour mixture with remaining ingredients in a bowl. Season to taste.

5   Place a wok over high heat. Add oil and heat until almost smoking. Stir-fry duck briefly, then transfer to a plate. Pour oil from wok into a heat-proof bowl, leaving 1 tbs in wok.

6   Reheat oil in wok until hot but not smoking. Add garlic, chilli and ginger and stir-fry for 20 seconds. Add pineapple and stir-fry for 30 seconds. Add duck pieces and Chinese wine and stir-fry for 20 seconds.

7   Add noodles and sauce. Stir until well combined, taking care not to break up the noodles. Add spring onions. Check seasoning and adjust if necessary. Serve.

Note Ho fun are wide, flat rice noodles, available from Asian food shops.

# Justine's quail with port and eschalot sauce

Serves 2
Preparation time: 20 mins
Cooking time: about 1 hour

2 quail
⅓ cup (80 ml) olive oil
4 eschalots, finely sliced
1 cup (250 ml) ruby port
1 tsp caster sugar
½ cup (125 ml) veal glaze
5 kipfler potatoes (or any
  other waxy potato)
¼ cup duck fat
2 carrots, peeled and grated
¾ cup (185 ml) chicken stock
1 tbs chervil leaves, to garnish

Justine says: 'This dish has been in my family for many years. I even remember my grandmother telling me that her mother would cook quails this way! I have adapted this dish in many ways. The port and eschalot sauce goes well with roasted pork neck, poussin and even rabbit, and sautéed cabbage or lentils are both great accompaniments instead of potatoes. The beauty of this quail dish is the "one pot" cooking technique. The sauce becomes rich and full-bodied because the meat braises in its juices, the port and eschalots. This is definitely worth a try for a dinner party or even a Sunday dinner in winter.'

Method

1   Trim quail and pat dry with absorbent paper. Tie legs of quail using kitchen string and season with salt and pepper. Heat 2 tbs oil in a large saucepan. Add quail and cook, turning, for 3–4 mins or until evenly browned all over. Remove from pan. Set aside.

2   Add eschalots to the same pan. Cook for 4–5 mins or until softened and caramelised. Return quail to pan with port and sugar. Cook for about 2 mins to reduce a little. Add veal glaze. Reduce heat and simmer, covered, for 40 mins, until quail is tender, adding 1 tbs water if sauce becomes too thick.

3   Meanwhile, peel and cut potatoes in 2 cm cubes. Heat 2 tbs duck fat and remaining oil in a frying pan over high heat. Add potatoes and sauté for 15 mins, adjusting heat as necessary until potatoes are crisp and tender. Season with salt.

4   For the carrot puree, melt remaining duck fat in a saucepan and add grated carrots, salt and pepper. Cook, stirring, for 2 mins. Add stock. Cook until the carrots are soft. Strain most of the liquid, then, using a stick blender, blend carrot until nice and smooth. To get a glossier and more refined texture put this puree through a sieve.

5   To serve, smear carrot puree over serving plate. Remove quail from pan, discard string. I like to leave the quail whole; however, you can halve or quarter them if you wish, for presentation. Arrange quail and potatoes. Serve with eschalot and port reduction. Garnish with chervil.

# Donovan Cooke's slow-cooked pigeon

At the Hong Kong Jockey Club, Julie came up against world-renowned chef Donovan Cooke and his protégé, Tam Kin Pak, in the celebrity chef challenge. When Donovan unveiled the dish – slow-cooked pigeon with Périgord black truffles, confit legs, tortellini of wild mushrooms, celeriac puree and baby leeks with a pigeon jus gras – Julie said she had never tasted anything like it. Donovan describes it as 'pure indulgence'. This recipe has been adapted slightly for home cooks who don't have access to a combi steamer, but it is still the ultimate in luxury. Julie had 90 minutes to cook the dish and a 15-minute head start on Pak. Without Donovan to coach you, you may need a little more time.

Serves 2
Preparation time: 1 hour 35 mins
Cooking time: 1 hour

**Pigeon in vacuum bag**
2 x 600 g Bresse pigeon (see note)
50 g Périgord black truffles
1 tsp (5 ml) port
1 tsp (5 ml) madeira
1 tsp (5 ml) Armagnac

**Confit legs**
reserved pigeon legs
2 garlic cloves, chopped
1 tsp thyme leaves, chopped
10 g sea salt
100 g duck fat

**Pigeon jus gras**
100 g pigeon bones
2 tbs corn oil
2 eschalots, sliced
2 button mushrooms, sliced
⅓ cup (80 ml) madeira
1¼ cups (310 ml) chicken stock
1 tsp thyme leaves
20 g cold butter, chopped

**Celeriac puree**
20 g butter
200 g celeriac, peeled and
  grated
¾ cup (180 ml) cream

**Tortellini**
1⅔ cup (250 g) plain flour
1 tbs salt
4 egg yolks
1 egg
1½ tbs olive oil
50 g wild mushrooms, sliced
1 eschalot, finely chopped
1 tsp chopped chives
olive oil, extra

**Baby leeks**
2 tbs olive oil
4 baby leeks
½ cup (125 ml) chicken stock

Method

1   Preheat oven to 100°C (80° fan-forced). To prepare the pigeon, remove the head, feet and legs, reserving the legs for the confit, then cut out the wishbone and remove the intestines. Run your fingers under the neck skin and breast to make a pocket. Slice half of the truffle thinly and place between the skin and the flesh. Place the 2 pigeons into a vacuum pack bag and add the port, madeira, Armagnac, salt and pepper, then vacuum on full power. Place the pigeon into a combi steamer at 80°C with half-fan for 3 mins, then change to 65°C for 25 mins. Remove from the combi steamer and allow to rest. (For the home cook, place a large piece of baking paper over a piece of foil. Place the pigeons on the baking paper. Drizzle with port, madeira and Armagnac. Season. Wrap paper and foil around to form a parcel, then place the parcel in a large steamer. Steam, covered, for 10 mins. Turn off heat. Stand in steamer, covered, until ready to use.)

2   To make the confit legs, remove the thigh bone from the pigeon legs. Combine the garlic, thyme and sea salt, and rub into the legs. Allow to sit for 20 mins, then wipe off the salt mixture. Heat the duck fat in a saucepan and add the legs. Cook over low heat, turning occasionally for 30 mins, until tender. Remove the legs from the fat and pan-fry until the skin is crispy. Keep in a warm place.

3   To make the jus gras, chop the pigeon bones. Heat the corn oil in a frying pan and cook the bones over medium-high heat until golden brown. Add the eschalots and mushrooms and cook until lightly caramelised. Deglaze the pan with madeira. Cook until reduced by half. Add the chicken stock, 1¼ cups (310 ml) of water and the thyme, and bring to the boil. Cook over high heat for 30–40 mins. Strain the sauce into a bowl, then sit the bowl in iced water. When the sauce has set, scrape off the fat and discard. Reduce the stock again by half, then season to taste. Whisk in butter.

4   To make the tortellini, place the flour and salt into a food processor. With the motor running, add the egg yolks, egg and 1 tbs of the oil. Process to a crumbly texture, then tip out onto a floured workbench and knead into a smooth ball. Cover with cling film and rest in the refrigerator for 30 mins. Roll the pasta into thin sheets (or if using a pasta machine, roll to the thinnest setting), then cut into discs using

# Donovan Cooke's
# slow-cooked pigeon

a 9 cm round cutter. Heat the remaining olive oil in a frying pan and sauté the mushrooms and eschalot until soft. Season with salt and pepper and transfer to a plate to cool. Chop the mushroom mix finely and mix with the chives. Place ½ tsp of the mushroom mix in the centre of a pasta disc. Rub the rim of the disc with a little water and fold over to form a semicircle, pressing the edges to seal. Twist the two ends together to form a tortellini. Repeat with the remaining dough and filling. Cook in boiling salted water for 30 seconds, then place into iced water. When cold, remove from the water, toss with olive oil and set aside.

5    To make the celeriac puree, melt the butter in a frying pan and sweat the celeriac over medium heat until it starts to soften. Add the cream and cook until soft, then place into a blender and puree until smooth. Pass through a drum sieve, then season to taste. Pour into a plastic squeeze bottle and keep warm.

6    To cook the baby leeks, heat the olive oil in a frying pan and add the leeks and stock and cook over high heat until the liquid has evaporated and the leeks are soft and glazed. Season to taste and keep warm.

7    To finish, place the pigeon back into the combi steamer and cook at 60°C for 3 mins, then remove from the vacuum pack bag. (For the home cook, remove parcel from steamer and unwrap.) Add the juice to the sauce. Remove the breast from the bone and season with sea salt. Place the tortellini back into boiling salted water for 2 mins. Draw on the plate with the celeriac puree. Place the pigeon breast onto the plate with the confit legs, tortellini and baby leeks. Cut the remaining Périgord black truffles into batons and scatter over the pigeon. Drizzle the sauce over the dish to complete.

Note In Australia we use squab – ask your butcher or poultry supplier to source them for you.

# Seafood

Seafood secrets: shellfish, squid, snapper and salmon

# Josh's seafood secrets

Josh says: 'I'm a third-generation fishmonger. One of my earliest memories is going into the factory with my dad to unload a crab fisherman. I was so excited to see live crabs flicking around and biting onto anything that moved that I got a little too carried away and knocked over a full tub. Live crabs scattered all over the floor and of course one decides to latch onto my big toe. I still vividly remember sitting on the floor bawling my eyes out as my dad came running in his tight football shorts and singlet to save my toes. Even though it was a very sore event it is fair to say I was hooked on seafood then and there.

'If you want to eat really good seafood, the best thing you can do is to build a relationship with your local fishmonger. Always ask them what is in season and their personal choice for dinner tonight. I love it when a customer comes into my shop and says: "That fish you gave me last week was amazing. What do you recommend this week?" Australia has some of the best seafood in the world, so take advantage of what's in your own backyard and support the local fisheries.

'The most important thing about buying seafood is what you do with it once you've purchased it. There's no point going to the trouble of picking out the best seafood if you're going to leave it on the back seat of the car. The key factor in maintaining quality in seafood is temperature control. All fresh seafood should be kept between 0° and 4°C and frozen below −18°C. So always do your seafood shopping last and pack it in a cooler bag with ice. When you get home, put it in the coldest part of the fridge (the bottom shelf is generally the coldest), allowing for air circulation.

'Here are some handy Catalano family secrets that will make your seafood experience unforgettable.'

## Whole fish

When buying whole fish, the fish should have clear bulging eyes, not cloudy. The gills should be nice and red with no fishy smell. It's time to get your hands dirty – feel the fish, it should be nice and firm, and when touched it should spring back into shape. All the scales should be firmly attached and in good condition. The fish should look like it just came out of the water.

## Fillets

When selecting fillets, make sure there is no discolouration of the flesh. The flesh should be moist, with no unpleasant fishy smell. The bloodline (usually a red muscle band that runs through a fillet) should be appealing to the eye. If the portions are trimmed up and have minimal bloodlines, it generally means your fishmonger takes pride in what they do and looks after the fish they sell.

## Shellfish

Lobsters, crabs, bugs and prawns are crowd favourites and show stoppers. I would always recommend buying shellfish raw and cooking them yourself. They should have a fresh ocean smell to them and no discolouration of the joints. When they start to go black in the joints and segments, it means the product is starting to deteriorate. As a general rule, prawns are caught and snap-frozen at sea, because the fishing grounds are so remote, though this depends on the area where you're purchasing your seafood. Unless your fishmonger has told you that the prawns are truly fresh (and have never been frozen), I would suggest you stick to frozen prawns. You can compare prices for shellfish by asking for the 'count per pound'. The lower the count, the larger the size of the individual shellfish – and the larger the size, the higher the price.

## Mussels

If you're looking for a great dish on a budget, you can't go past mussels. Although seasons vary, mussels are harvested all over Australia, so fresh live mussels are available all year round. When the mussel is alive it holds ocean water inside it, but after spending time out of the ocean it releases that water and starts to die. If a mussel has started to open, the best way to see if it is still alive is to tap it with another mussel. If it starts to close, it means it's alive and ready to be cooked.

## Oysters

Fresh oysters can be done many different ways, but are often simply enjoyed clean and natural. If you enjoy eating the freshest oysters, I would suggest you duck out to the shops and invest in an oyster knife. Shucking oysters looks and sounds tricky, but if you have the right tools there's not much to it. (Check out 'How to shuck an oyster' on page 117.) Select oysters that are heavy, firmly closed and don't sound hollow when tapped with the handle of a knife. If this all sounds a bit too hard and you prefer to buy shucked oysters, always ask your fishmonger when they were opened. Then pick out the ones that look plump and juicy, with no discolouration in the flesh. The meat should cover most of the shell. I believe an oyster should be eaten moments after it's opened, but they will keep for seven days.

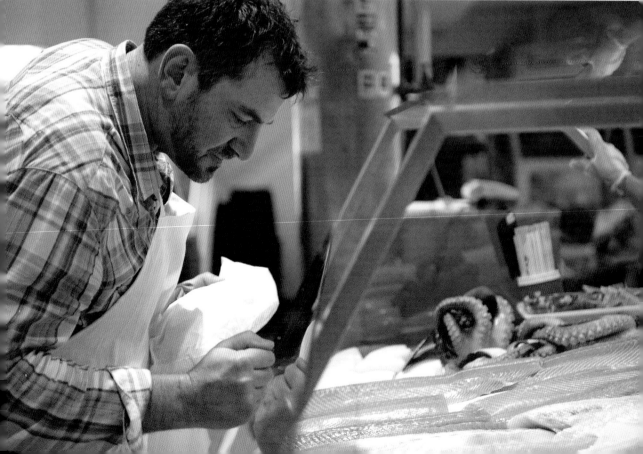

# How to shuck an oyster

**1**

Place the oyster on a tea towel with the flat side facing up, and the hinge (the pointy bit where the upper shell meets the lower part) of the oyster pointing towards you. Fold the towel back over the oyster and hold tightly, applying pressure down. Place your knife in at the hinge and apply pressure.

**2**

Twist and wriggle the blade until the knife enters the oyster and the lid pops up. Slide the knife along the top lid and remove the lid.

**3**

Turn the oyster around and slide the knife underneath the oyster and cut it away from the shell. Clean away any bits of shell that may have chipped off and the oyster is ready.

# How to fillet a fish

1

Take a whole fish that has been gutted and scaled. Pat dry with absorbent paper so it isn't too slippery. Using a sharp knife, make a cut on a 55° angle, just behind the gills and under the fin, where the head meets the body. Score through the flesh on both sides, then cut right through the bone to remove the head.

2

Cut along the backbone, feeling where the flesh joins the bone, easing to lift the meat from the ribs. Cut at the tail end to release the flesh from the tail.

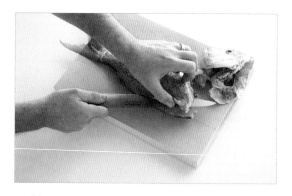

3

At the top of the spine, cut through the small bones that attach the flesh.

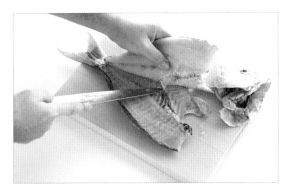

4
Lift off the fillet. Repeat with the other side.

5
Lay the fillets outside down and cut a sliver from the top of the fillet to remove the tiny belly bones. Run your knife over the skin to make sure no scales remain.

6
To pin bone the fish, feel where the small ribs are and pull out with tweezers. Support the flesh with your fingertips so you don't tear it.

# How to prepare squid

1

Pull the tentacles firmly to separate the head from the tube. Try not to break the ink sac, as the ink will stain.

2

Remove the quill (the see-through plastic-like feather inside the hood).

3

Pull the wings from the tube to loosen the skin.

4

Pull off all the skin.

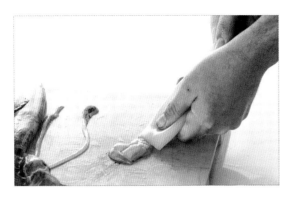

5

Lay the tube on the board and use your hand to press from the tip, pushing out any remaining insides.

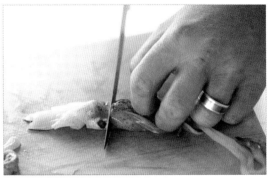

6

Cut below the eyes and discard the head and guts.

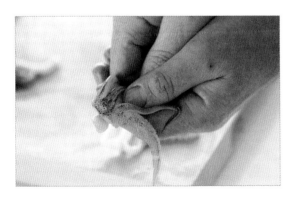

7

Push the beak (mouth) out from between the tentacles, and discard the beak. Reserve the tentacles.

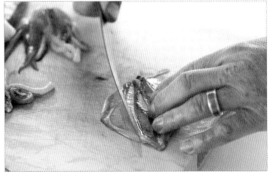

8

Lay out the wings and cut the cartilage from the edge (you will feel it with your fingers). Use a knife to scrape the skin from the wing.

# How to crack open a crab

1

Be prepared to make a mess – wear an apron or a bib! Dig your thumb below the eyes of the cooked crab and break through the shell.

2

Clean the crab, removing the 'dead man's fingers' – the crab's filtration system, which looks like grey tubes.

3

Remove the V-shaped underbelly flap.

4

Split the body in two.

5

Extract the meat from the two halves of the body.

6

Crack the claw to extract the last of the meat.

# How to extract a lobster's meat

1

Twist the head and tail of the cooked lobster in opposite directions.

2

Remove the tail fins and gently break the shell, trying not to break off or tear any of the flesh.

3

Extract the tail meat in one piece.

4

Separate the top from the bottom of the body, remove the legs and break open the joints where the legs meet the body.

5

Pick the meat out of the joints and then break open the legs and extract the meat.

6

Using a mallet, break open the antennae to get the meat from them.

# André's breaded oysters

André chose the core ingredients for the romance-themed invention test and prepared breaded oysters as an entrée to a three-course meal intended to win Gary, George and Matt's favour. He told the cameras: 'I think Italian food is pretty sexy if it's done right', but then he turned the griller up too high. It wasn't the judges' hearts he set on fire, but the oysters. Be sure to watch yours carefully! André served his oysters before a main of polenta with Balmain bugs. The recipe for his polenta dish is on page 148.

Makes 6 large oysters
Preparation time: 15 mins
Cooking time: 5 mins

3 slices white bread, crusts
  removed, roughly torn
25 g butter
2 anchovy fillets, finely chopped
olive oil
zest and juice of 1 lemon
2 tbs finely chopped parsley
1 small tomato, peeled, seeded
  and finely diced
6 large oysters, shucked (reserve
  and clean 6 half shells)
rock salt, to serve
lemon cheek, to serve

'Very delicate. You get that
nice saltiness of the oyster, the
creaminess of the oyster, then
the toasty herby crumbs on top
and the little bits of tomato at
the end. And it doesn't taste
burnt! You must have caught
them just in time.' – Gary to
André, after he had tasted
his dish

Method

1   Preheat the oven grill until hot.

2   Process the bread in a food processor to make fine breadcrumbs.

3   Combine the butter, anchovies and a drizzle of olive oil in a frying pan. Cook over medium heat until the butter has melted. Add the breadcrumbs and cook, stirring, until lightly golden. Stir in the lemon zest and juice, the parsley and the tomato.

4   Line a baking tray with foil, place the oysters on the tray and top with the breadcrumb mixture. Cook under the grill for 20–30 seconds, to warm through.

5   Arrange the clean oyster shells on a serving plate lined with rock salt. Place the oysters into the shells, and serve with a lemon cheek on the side.

# Pressure test paella

Sandra, Julie and Aaron were the three contestants cooking for their lives in the paella pressure test. Gary told them they'd be working from an old family recipe belonging to his friend, Spanish chef Miguel Cascales Maestre. Sandra was happy, saying: 'I've cooked paella so many times, it's going to come from the heart.' When she tasted it, that all changed. The first thing she thought was: 'My god, where are the prawns? Where is the chicken, and where is the pork?' It wasn't the paella she'd grown up with.

George told them the key to success was tasting as they went, to adjust the balance of flavours. Cooking the rice would also be crucial: 'If the rice isn't cooked, it can be crunchy. If the rice is overcooked, it will be soggy like porridge. And that crust is extremely important on the bottom of the pan.' Matt had some stern words for them too: 'Bring us a paella without that crust and you risk going home. Bring us a paella that is soupy, and I will personally open the car door and send you home myself.'

They had just 35 minutes to cook the dish. Things didn't run smoothly, of course, and there were tears along the way. As the contestants plated up at the end, spectator Sam noted that the three paellas were different colours: 'Sandra's looked almost bright red, Julie's looked quite dark and Aaron's was lighter than them both.' It was as though the same recipe had produced three different dishes.

Aaron was the unlucky one sent home – but not because his paella was soupy. On the contrary, Gary said his crust was fabulous, the best of all of them, and just made him want to 'tuck in'. Unfortunately, Aaron hadn't tasted the dish often enough as he cooked, so it wasn't as gutsy and flavoursome as it could have been. With the offer of an apprenticeship in one of George's restaurants, though, Aaron was moving closer towards achieving his dream even as he left the MasterChef kitchen for good.

Miguel Cascales Maestre's original recipe is made with Calasparra rice and piquillo peppers. Although these ingredients are available from Spanish delicatessens or specialty suppliers, this recipe uses different ingredients, more readily available in Australian shops.

# Pressure test paella

Serves 2–3
Preparation time: 30 mins
Cooking time: 30 mins +
    5 mins resting

2 tbs olive oil

1¾ cups (350 g) short
    grain rice

4 cups (1 litre) fish stock

18 small mussels, scrubbed
    and debearded

200 g fresh or frozen peas

1 lemon, cut into wedges

1 lime, cut into wedges

### Sofrito

¼ cup (60 ml) extra virgin
    olive oil

2 tsp sherry vinegar

1 large ripe tomato, coarsely
    chopped

2 garlic cloves, coarsely chopped

1 eschalot, coarsely chopped

1 chargrilled red capsicum

6 large stems thyme, leaves
    picked

½ cup mint leaves (about
    ¼ bunch)

½ cup coarsely chopped
    coriander leaves and stems
    (about ¼ bunch)

½ bunch chives, coarsely
    chopped

½ cup flat-leaf parsley,
    coarsely chopped,

1 pinch saffron

1 tsp sweet paprika

1 tsp smoked paprika

## Method

1   To make the sofrito, blend the oil, vinegar, tomato, garlic, eschalot
    and capsicum in a blender or food processor until smooth. Add the
    herbs and spices, blend again and season with salt to taste.

2   Place a paella pan on the stove over high heat, add the olive oil and
    cook the rice for 1 min until it changes colour.

3   Add ¾ cup of the sofrito paste and cook over high heat for 1 min,
    stirring until evenly combined with the rice. Add the stock and bring
    to the boil, then add the mussels. Cook uncovered for 25 mins over
    high heat. When the dish is ready, the stock will have evaporated, the
    rice will be tender, and a delicious crust will form on the base of the
    pan. Remove from the heat, fold through the peas and cook them
    with the residual heat in the pan.

4   Cover with a clean tea towel and rest for 5 mins. Serve warm, not
    steaming hot. Squeeze half the lemon and lime over the paella and
    season to taste before serving straight from the pan. Garnish with
    remaining lemon and lime wedges.

# Alex Herbert's potato gnocchi with sautéed prawns in a burnt-butter sauce

In the celebrity chef challenge, Chris cooked off against Alex Herbert, head chef and co-owner of Sydney's Bird Cow Fish. Alex had chosen one of her signature dishes – potato gnocchi with sautéed prawns in a burnt-butter sauce. 'Gnocchi is a death dish,' Matt told Chris. 'It's the dish I'm always going to order when I walk into a restaurant because it tells you where the chef sits.' Chris confessed that the last time he'd made gnocchi it had turned out like potato soup. Sam said it was the first time he'd ever seen Chris actually look nervous – 'It's good to know the ice man can melt a bit.'

Chris tasted the dish and commented on how beautifully light the gnocchi were. Alex explained that the recipe had two parts – making the gnocchi, then cooking them and combining them with the burnt-butter verjuice sauce – and that timing would be crucial. When Sarah asked Alex what could go wrong, she replied, 'Everything.'

With a half-hour head start, Chris had time for a few test runs after he'd made his gnocchi, while Alex plated up with only seconds to spare. The judges concurred that Chris had done an excellent job, producing a dish with a dark, rich, salty intensity, but declared Alex's offering the winner, as it was 'much more alive', with prawns that pinged and popped in the mouth.

Serves 6
Preparation time: 45 mins
Cooking time: 1 hour

1.5 kg desiree potatoes
1 egg (55 g)
2 tbs grated grana parmesan
2 tsp sea salt
¾ cup (105 g) plain flour
60 g unsalted butter
300 g fresh prawn meat (about 600 g green king prawns)
¼ cup verjuice
6 tsp salted baby capers, rinsed and drained
¼ cup finely chopped flat-leaf parsley

Sage butter
200 g unsalted butter, diced
1 bunch sage, leaves picked

'I've eaten this dish at Bird Cow Fish, and it's a cracker – the way those prawns pop in your mouth, and the pillows of gnocchi . . . There's a bit of spring as you bite into them, then – pffff! – magically, they're gone.' – Matt

# Alex Herbert's potato gnocchi with sautéed prawns in a burnt-butter sauce

Method

1   Place the unpeeled potatoes in a large saucepan of cold water and bring to the boil. Reduce the heat and simmer for 30 mins or until tender. The potatoes must be neither under- nor overcooked. Test with a skewer – when it is easily inserted, they are cooked (avoid testing too frequently or they may become waterlogged).

2   Drain the potatoes into a colander, cover with a clean tea towel and place the colander over the original saucepan in a warm place for 10 mins to drain completely.

3   Peel the potatoes and pass through a mouli, in batches, into the original dry saucepan. Gently mix in the egg, parmesan and salt. Sift the flour over, and combine with a few swift folds. Tip the mixture onto a lightly floured bench and gently work it into a smooth mound.

4   Using a pastry scrape, scrape down the bench, wash and dry your hands and lightly flour the surface again. Take a quarter of the potato mixture at a time and roll out into a sausage shape about 1.5 cm thick. Cut each sausage into 2 cm pieces. Repeat with remaining mixture to make about 60 pieces. Place onto a tray lined with baking paper.

5   To make the sage butter, melt the butter in a shallow frying pan. When starting to bubble, add the sage leaves and cook until crisp and almost translucent. Pour through a sieve placed over a bowl. Spread the leaves on paper towel to drain and keep warm. Reserve the butter.

6   When ready to cook the gnocchi, melt 20 g of the butter in a wide frying pan and cook until it becomes nut brown. Add 100 g of the prawn meat and sauté for 1 min. Deglaze with a dash of verjuice and add 2 tsp of capers.

7   Cook the gnocchi in a large pan of boiling salted water in batches of 20 at a time. Shortly after the gnocchi has risen to the surface (test to see if it is cooked) remove with a strainer, drain and add to the frying pan. Toss the pan to coat the gnocchi in the butter. Season with salt and pepper and add 1 tbs of the chopped parsley. Spoon among 2 serving plates and top with fried sage leaves. Deglaze the pan with a little of the reserved sage butter and pour over the finished gnocchi. Repeat twice to complete 6 serves.

# Emmanuel Stroobant's scampi with pine mushrooms and potatoes

Emmanuel Stroobant is executive chef at Saint Pierre, Singapore, and owns a string of restaurants. He has written two cookbooks, *Cuisine Unplugged* and *Vine Dining*, and has his own TV series, *Chef in Black*. André faced him in the celebrity chef challenge. Looking back, André comments: 'When Emmanuel Stroobant's dish was revealed to me it took a while to comprehend, as there was so much happening on the plate. The recipe asked for "turned" potato – a new technique I had to learn quick smart. The potato tuille was also new to me: it had an intense potato chip flavour with a feather-like texture. The bisque is fantastic, with a deep, rich flavour that binds extremely well with the fresh scampi and mushroom.'

## Method

1. To make the turned potatoes, use a small sharp knife to trim the potatoes into a barrel shape. Place the potatoes in a large saucepan of cold water. Bring to the boil. Cook until just tender. When ready to serve, melt the butter in a large saucepan. Remove from the heat, then add the potatoes and chives and toss to combine.

2. Heat 1 tbs of the olive oil in a large frying pan. Add reserved scampi heads and shells, onion, garlic, leek and fennel. Cook, stirring, until onion is soft. Add half the tomato and 4 cups (1 litre) water. Bring to the boil and simmer, uncovered, for 45 mins. Strain the stock through a fine sieve placed over a clean saucepan and simmer, uncovered, for a further 15 mins

3. Heat 1 tbs of the remaining olive oil in a frying pan and cook the eschalots and mushrooms until just soft. Add ½ cup (125 ml) water and bring to the boil. Strain mixture. Reserve mushrooms and cooking liquid.

4. Place the port in a saucepan and simmer until reduced to a syrup. Add ⅔ cup (160 ml) scampi stock and ⅔ cup (160 ml) mushroom liquid. Bring to the boil and reduce for 2 mins, then season to taste. Add 2 tbs of the cream and bring to a boil. Gradually whisk in 30 g of the butter and the lemon juice until emulsified. Add half the walnut oil and blend with a stick blender.

5. Put the potatoes through a juicer. Line a sieve with a double layer of muslin, then place it over a bowl and strain the potato juice, discarding the solids in the muslin. Heat a non-stick frying pan over low heat. Whisk potato juice. Pour a little juice into the pan to create a thin layer. Cook for a minute until the water has evaporated and starch is beginning to brown, leaving a thin 'tuille'. Remove from heat to allow tuille to continue cooking from the heat of the pan and become crisp. Season with salt.

6. Heat the remaining butter in a large frying pan and cook the reserved mushrooms over high heat until golden. Remove from heat. Add half the chives and toss to combine.

7. Cook the scampi in batches in a large oiled non-stick frying pan for 30 seconds. Drizzle with the remaining walnut oil.

8. Combine the remaining tomato with remaining olive oil, chives and 2 tsp of remaining scampi stock.

9. Arrange 5 small stacks of eschalot and mushroom mixture on warm serving plates, as pictured. Top with tomato mixture. Arrange scampi and potatoes alternately in between. Drizzle with sauce and garnish with chives and potato tuille. Serve immediately.

Serves 4
Preparation time: 45 mins
Cooking time: 1 hour 20 mins

¼ cup (60 ml) olive oil
12 scampi, peeled and deveined (reserve heads and shells)
1 onion, finely chopped
6 garlic cloves, crushed
1 leek, finely chopped
1 bulb fennel, diced
2 vine-ripened tomatoes, peeled, seeded and diced
2 eschalots, finely chopped
2 pine mushrooms, wiped with damp paper towel, cut into 2 cm pieces
⅓ cup (80 ml) white port
¼ cup (60 ml) cream
50 g cold butter, diced
1 tbs lemon juice
¼ cup (60 ml) walnut oil
3 large potatoes, peeled
2 tbs finely chopped chives

Turned potatoes
12 small potatoes
60 g butter
3 tbs finely chopped chives

# Chargrilled stuffed squid

A killer squid was Michelle, Sam and Kate's nemesis when they came up short in the Chinese invention test and had to fight to keep their places in the competition.

The judges looked for tenderness in the squid, and caramelised golden char marks. Points were also awarded for a nice bright colour in the tomato, a black glossiness to the olives and a citric zing in the stuffing. Points were deducted for a lack of generosity in the stuffing, undercooking the squid – and olive pips. ('That olive pip looked like the nail in my coffin to me,' Sam said when Matt handed it back to him.)

The three attempts were all close, each with its own strengths and weaknesses, but it was Michelle who was eliminated. Gary said her dish didn't have enough stuffing, and Matt said it lacked the fresh lemon zing they were looking for.

## Method

1   Clean the squid following the instructions on page 120. Wash the tube out. Roughly chop the tentacles.

2   Heat 1½ tbs of the olive oil in a frying pan. Cook the anchovies, garlic and eschalots until soft. Add the tentacles and cook just until opaque. Season to taste. Combine the tentacle mixture in a bowl with the lemon rind and juice, parsley and breadcrumbs.

3   Spoon mixture into the squid hoods, leaving 1 cm at the end to secure with a toothpick. Drizzle with a little extra oil. Heat a grill-pan and cook the squid over medium-high heat, turning occasionally, until golden and just cooked through. Slice the squid.

4   Meanwhile, combine the tomato, beans, olives, vinegar and the remaining oil in a bowl and season to taste. Divide the salad among serving plates and top with squid. Spoon over any remaining dressing to serve.

Serves 2
Preparation time: 35 mins
Cooking time: 10 mins

2 whole squid (800 g)
2 tbs olive oil, plus extra oil to drizzle
2 anchovy fillets
1 clove garlic, finely chopped
2 eschalots, finely chopped
1 tsp finely grated lemon rind
1 tbs lemon juice
1–2 tbs coarsely chopped fresh flat-leaf parsley
½ cup (20 g) fresh ciabatta or sourdough breadcrumbs
1 vine-ripened tomato, blanched, peeled, seeded, and diced
100 g green beans, blanched and refreshed in cold water
½ cup (80 g) pitted kalamata olives
2 tbs sherry vinegar

Recipe by Kate Nichols

# Brent's Top Fifty salt and pepper squid

Brent says: 'Armed with four hours of restless sleep I staggered into the cold lights of Victoria Markets on the morning of my audition. I did not know what I wanted, but I was looking for something insanely fresh, quick to cook and tasty, and above all, something that the judges would love.

'And there they were, being laid on the ice for the first time. When the squids' eyes sparkle at you under the fridge cabinet lights, you know they are fresh.

'I took the squid and waltzed with excitement around the awaking market to find partners for them. Fresh coriander, red chilli, limes, bean shoots, mint and a red capsicum for a Thai-style salad – that should do the trick. This recipe is as simple as it is tasty. Making something flashy and gussying it up does not make it taste any better. Just serve it in a spirit of honesty and generosity. This dish will be a huge hit for you, as it was for me. Top 50 and beyond!'

Serves 2
Preparation time: 15 mins
Cooking time: 5 mins

½ cup (75 g) cornflour
½ cup (75 g) rice flour
½ tsp sea salt
½ tsp cracked black pepper
½ tsp Chinese five-spice
½ tsp of ground coriander
2 squid, cleaned
1 tsp fish sauce
oil for deep-frying
2 eggwhites, lightly whisked

Dressing
1 tbs lime juice
1 tsp grated palm sugar
1 tsp fish sauce
½ long red chilli, seeded,
  chopped finely

Salad
2 cups bean shoots, washed
1 cup washed and picked mint
  leaves
1 cup washed coriander stems
  and leaves
1 red capsicum, thinly sliced

Method

1   To make the dressing, stir lime juice, palm sugar and fish sauce in a small jug until sugar dissolves. Stir in chilli.

2   Combine flours, salt, pepper, spice and coriander in a medium bowl.

3   Cut the squid tube lengthways and open out flat. Lightly scrape inside with a sharp knife to remove the translucent film (this can make it tough and chewy). Wash and pat dry.

4   Using a sharp knife, score inside in a criss-cross pattern. Cut each piece in half lengthways. Cut each strip crossways into 4 pieces. Clean the tentacles and chop to similar lengths. Place squid in a small bowl with fish sauce. Stir to combine.

5   Heat oil in a wok or medium saucepan. Dip squid in eggwhites, then in the flour mixture. Shake off excess flour. Cook squid in batches, until golden.

6   Combine salad ingredients in a small bowl.

7   Drizzle squid with half the dressing. Serve with salad and remaining dressing.

# Guy Grossi's insalata di arrigosta con insalata ruselle

Serves 2
Preparation time: 30 mins
Cooking time: 30 mins

1 small beetroot, peeled
  and diced
1½ tbs white wine or
  chardonnay vinegar
2 tbs caster sugar
white vinegar
2 quail eggs
1 rock lobster, cooked and
  prepared (see page 124)
4 slices bottarga (sun-dried
  mullet roe)
watercress sprigs, to serve
olive oil

Russian salad

2 large spunta potatoes
  (or other variety), peeled
½ small carrot, peeled and diced
¼ cup (35 g) shelled peas
2 tbs mayonnaise (see page 28)
½ tsp grated horseradish
sea salt and freshly ground
  black pepper

Guy Grossi, owner and chef of Grossi Florentino in Melbourne, says: 'I love to cook because it keeps me in touch with my Italian heritage and allows me to express myself.' Justine went head to head with him in the celebrity chef challenge. Guy had chosen to make *insalata di arrigosta con insalata ruselle*, or lobster with Russian salad – an intricate, delicate dish with clean flavours.

Guy told Justine the lobster was paramount. If it wasn't cooked correctly, the dish would collapse, because 'everything else just becomes incidental'. As George noted, if you overcook lobster, it turns into rubber. Justine took this warning too much to heart, perhaps, as her lobster was underdone, and she lost the challenge, but Guy told her she had the makings of a great chef.

Method

1   To make the Russian salad, place the potatoes in a saucepan of cold water. Bring to the boil, reduce the heat and cook until almost tender. Add the carrot and peas. Boil about 5 mins or until vegetables are tender. Drain and cool completely. Cut the potatoes into small dice about the same size as the carrot. Mix with the carrot, peas, mayonnaise and horseradish. Season to taste. You may need to add a little more mayonnaise if the mixture is too dry.

2   Meanwhile, place the beetroot, wine and sugar in a small saucepan and cook until tender. Drain beetroot, reserving liquid.

3   Half fill a small frying pan with water, add a splash of white vinegar and bring to the boil. Reduce the heat until barely simmering. Using a slotted spoon, swirl the water around to make a whirlpool. Gently crack 1 quail egg into a cup, taking care not to break the yolk. Tip the egg into the pan and cook for 2 mins. Remove and drain on absorbent paper. Keep warm while you repeat with remaining egg.

4   To serve, spoon some Russian salad into the centre of each plate. On top of this put some lobster meat from the legs. Cut the tail meat into 5 mm thick medallions. Arrange a few slices of tail meat on top, then add a quail egg and 2 slices of bottarga. Drizzle the beetroot reduction around the plate, scatter over a few watercress sprigs and drizzle with a little oil.

# Lucas's Singapore chilli mud crab

Lucas says: 'Gary and Matt both love Singapore chilli mud crab. It's one of their favourite dishes. To have them tell me this was among the best they'd ever had was just amazing. It was on the strength of this dish that I made it into the Top Fifty and through to the next round of the competition. It was also chilli mud crab that brought my wife and I together – we ordered it on our first night out.'

Method

1  Cook mud crab in boiling salted water for 15 mins. Drain. Refresh in iced water.

2  To make the chilli base, use a mortar and pestle to pound the chillies, garlic and ginger to a paste. Add 1 tbs of the peanut oil and combine well.

3  To make the chilli sauce, combine all the ingredients in a small bowl.

4  Prepare the crab by lifting the tail flap and easing off the back shell. Remove and discard the gills, liver and brain matter, and rinse the crab well. Using a cleaver or heavy knife, cut the crab into four pieces.

5  Heat the oil in a wok until hot and smoking. Add the chilli base and stir for 30 seconds. Add the crab pieces and cook for 30 seconds, stirring continuously, then add the chilli sauce and cook, uncovered, for 5 mins, or until sauce thickens slightly. Season with salt and pepper.

6  To serve, arrange the crab in a large bowl, then pour over the sauce. Scatter with coriander leaves and serve with lime wedges.

Serves 2
Preparation time: 20 mins
Cooking time: about 6 mins

1 mud crab (1.25–1.5 kg)
2 tbs peanut oil
coriander leaves and lime
  wedges, to serve

Chilli base
2 fresh small red chillies,
  coarsely chopped
2 large garlic cloves, coarsely
  chopped
10 g piece fresh ginger, peeled
  and coarsely chopped
1 tbs peanut oil

Chilli sauce
1 cup (250 ml) tomato paste
30 g coarsely grated palm sugar,
  dissolved in $\frac{1}{3}$ cup (80 ml)
  warm water
juice of 2 limes
$\frac{1}{4}$ cup (60 ml) tomato sauce
$\frac{3}{4}$–1 tbs black bean sauce,
  to taste

# Melissa's bug and sage tortellini

Melissa says: 'I cook to taste, so the quantities of the seasonings I give here are really only a guide. The idea is that the bug meat is super-fresh and the herbs don't overpower the taste of the bug, which is so delicate. I like my tortellini quite small and use an 8 cm cutter to cut the rings – about the size of a standard egg ring. When I cooked this dish for the judges at my audition, they suggested a hint of lemon zest would have been nice with it – maybe in the butter sauce.'

Serves 4
Preparation time: 30 mins +
  30 mins resting time
Cooking time: 6 mins

**Bechamel**
10 g butter
2 tsp plain flour
¼ cup milk

**Filling**
30 g butter
2–3 sage leaves, finely chopped
1 eschalot, finely chopped
1 cup fresh Balmain bug meat,
  finely chopped
1 tbs fresh breadcrumbs (if
  needed to thicken the mixture)

**Pasta dough**
½ quantity pasta dough
  (see page 31)

**Butter and sage sauce**
75 g butter
12 sage leaves
½ tsp lemon zest

## Method

1   To make the bechamel, melt butter in a small saucepan. Add flour and stir until mixture thickens and bubbles. Gradually stir in milk. Cook until mixture boils and thickens. Remove from heat.

2   To make the filling, melt the butter in a frying pan and add the sage and eschalot. Cook over medium heat until the eschalot is soft, then add the bug meat and cook just until opaque. Add the bechamel and breadcrumbs. Cool.

3   Make one quantity of pasta dough (see recipe on page 31) – and then roll it out.

4   To make the tortellini, use an 8 cm round cutter to cut circles from the pasta dough. Keep the dough covered with cling film or a clean tea towel as you work so it doesn't dry out. Place about a half tsp of the filling onto each round. Fold in half and press the edges together. It is essential all the air is pressed out of the tortellini and that the edges are well sealed. If the dough starts to dry out, use water at the edges to help stick them together. Bring the edges of the dough together around your little finger, pressing the edges together, twisting up. Firmly press the outer edges, perfecting the shape as you finish each tortellini.

5   Bring a large pan of salted water to the boil. Cook the tortellini in batches for 3 mins.

6   To make the sauce, brown the butter in a large frying pan. Add the sage leaves and zest. Drain the tortellini and add to the pan. Toss to coat in the sauce.

# André's loose polenta and semolina with bug bisque

André says: 'This was my favourite dish that I made during the competition. It contributed to my victory in the romance-themed invention test. I was very proud of how well it came together, with the silkiness of the polenta and semolina and the richness and depth of flavour of the bug bisque. It is a sensual dish that will win many hearts.'

Serves 2
Preparation time: 20 mins
Cooking time: about 1 hour

3 Balmain bugs
¼ cup (60 ml) olive oil
1 onion, roughly chopped
1 garlic clove, sliced
1 fennel bulb, roughly chopped
1 tbs roughly chopped parsley
  stems
1 tomato, roughly chopped
2 tbs tomato paste
¼ cup (60 ml) ouzo
¼ cup (60 ml) white wine
¼ cup (45 g) semolina
¼ cup (45 g) polenta
2 cups (500 ml) fish stock
60 g unsalted butter
1 garlic clove, finely chopped
2 tbs chopped parsley
2 tbs milk

Method

1   Remove tails from bugs and cut meat into thick slices. Reserve shells.

2   Heat 2 tbs of the oil in a frying pan over a medium-high heat. Add the reserved bug shells and fry for 2–3 mins until nicely toasted. Cook the onion and garlic for 2 mins, then add the fennel and parsley stalks and cook for a further 3 mins, until soft. Add the chopped tomato and tomato paste. Cook on a low heat for about 5 mins, stirring occasionally, until it starts to caramelise. Deglaze with the ouzo and white wine. Reduce the heat slightly and simmer for 8 mins. Strain bisque through a muslin-lined sieve and discard solids.

3   Combine the semolina and polenta in a bowl. Bring 2 cups (500 ml) water and the stock to the boil in a saucepan. Reduce the heat so the water is simmering, and whisk in the semolina and polenta. Stir with a wooden spoon for a couple of minutes, then leave to cook over a low heat for 40 mins, stirring regularly. Season with salt and pepper.

4   Heat the remaining oil in a frying pan over high heat, and add half the butter. When it is foaming add the garlic, parsley and bug tail meat. Cook for 2–4 mins, until meat is opaque. Baste with the melted butter during cooking.

5   To finish the semolina, stir in the milk and remaining butter. Reheat the bisque.

6   To serve, spoon the semolina onto a serving plate, top with the Balmain bug tails and spoon the bisque around.

# Trevor's snapper fillet cooked en papillote

Serves 4
Preparation time: 15 mins
Cooking time: about 15 mins +
  3–4 mins resting

4 snapper fillets (640 g),
  skin off, ensure all bones
  have been removed
500 g unsalted butter
sea salt
⅓ cup (80 ml) white
  balsamic vinegar
1 medium onion, finely diced
1 garlic clove, finely diced
80 g pancetta, cut into batons
12 small brussels sprouts,
  trimmed and halved
2 cups (500 ml) chicken stock
micro-herbs or fennel tops,
  to garnish

Trevor says: 'Since leaving MasterChef I have quit my longstanding career in the navy and bought a restaurant called Capricci's in Rockingham, Western Australia. It has proven to be quite a challenge – but if everyone who walks out of Capricci's has a full belly and a smile on their face I will be a very happy man.

'Snapper fillet cooked en papillote with fancy brussels sprouts is a dish on our menu. To cook en papillote is to cook in a paper bag. This preserves the juices and ensures that the fish stays moist and absorbs all the flavours it is cooked with. I came up with this recipe after one of the masterclasses on the show. The white balsamic blends with the butter and the juices of the fish to create a fantastic flavour. It has fast become a family favourite and works well with all types of firm-fleshed fish. Bon appétit!'

Method

1   Preheat the oven to 180°C (160° fan-forced). Tear 4 sheets of foil about twice as long as a snapper fillet and cover with a sheet of non-stick baking paper. Place 100 g of butter on each sheet and season with sea salt and pepper. Place a snapper fillet on top of the butter and drizzle with 1 tbs of vinegar. Fold the paper and foil over the fillet, then seal the edges so no steam can escape. Place on a tray and bake for 10–12 mins, until the fillets are just cooked. (Cooking time will vary due to thickness and size of the fillets.) Remove the fillets from the oven and rest for 3–4 mins before serving.

2   Meanwhile, melt the remaining butter in a frying pan and sweat the onion and garlic for 2–3 mins until translucent but not coloured. Add the pancetta and fry for a further 2–3 mins. Add the brussels sprouts and toss them in the butter to coat. Add just enough chicken stock to half-cover the sprouts and cook over high heat for 4–5 mins until they are just tender but still have some crunch. Remove the sprouts from the cooking liquid. Boil the liquid until reduced by half to make a sauce.

3   Arrange the sprouts onto serving plates and drizzle over some of the reduced sauce. Remove the fish from the bag, being careful of the steam, and place in the centre of each plate. Take some of the liquid that has collected in the paper and drizzle it over the fish. Garnish with micro-herbs.

# Ceviche

The contestants lifted their mystery boxes one morning to find a whole snapper, eggs, potato, chilli and a beer. Sandra took these ingredients and prepared a ceviche, a traditional South American dish made from raw fish cut into bite-size pieces. Hers was the first plate the judges called up for tasting. Sandra says: 'When they called me to go up, I thought, wow, finally, *finally*, I'm getting something out there that they are interested in. The dish was a ceviche of snapper cooked in lemon juice, garlic and chilli. It's not cooked with heat – what the lemon does is the acidity goes through the actual fish and it cooks it. Choosing this dish was a risk, but it was one I had to take.'

Sandra served her ceviche in lemon boats, like those pictured left.

## Method

1   Cut lemons in half lengthways. Gently squeeze out juice into a small bowl. Reserve lemon halves to serve ceviche in.

2   Remove skin and cut fish into small cubes. Combine fish, juice, garlic and chilli in a small bowl. Refrigerate, covered, for 10 mins.

3   Meanwhile, using a vegetable peeler, slice potato into thin rounds.

4   Heat oil in a medium frying pan. Add the potato slices. Cook, turning, until browned and crisp. Drain on absorbent paper.

5   Spoon fish mixture into empty lemon halves. Garnish with coriander and serve with potato crisps.

Note The acid in the lemon juice marinade doesn't kill bacteria and parasites as heat would, so when you're making ceviche, it's important to start with the cleanest, freshest fish available.

## MasterTip
A Peruvian-style ceviche is usually garnished with thinly sliced onions and chillies and served with sweet potatoes and corn on the cob.

Serves 2
Preparation time: 20 mins

2 lemons
185 g snapper fillet
1 garlic clove, crushed
1 long red chilli, deseeded, finely diced
1 potato
2 tbs olive oil
coriander, to garnish

'The fish has got a lovely texture, nice hit of chilli, and very healthy. What are you trying to do, Sandra? I'm going to lose weight if I eat more of these dishes.'
– Gary

# Tom's lemon snapper swimming in a chilli and ginger sea

Serves 1
Preparation time: 10 mins
Cooking time: 20 mins

1 baby snapper (375 g),
  gutted and scaled
¼ cup plain flour
vegetable oil, for shallow frying
1 cm piece fresh ginger,
  julienned
1 garlic clove, julienned
1 spring onion, julienned
½ long red chilli, julienned
2 tsp vegetable oil, extra
1 tsp sesame oil
chopped coriander and
  Vietnamese mint, to garnish
soy sauce and lemon cheeks,
  to serve

'A very clever dish, beautifully
understated, and it looks
spectacular.' – Matt

Tom says: 'When I lifted the mystery box one day I saw, completely unexpected, an entire fish, and I was flooded with sudden memories of the Torres Strait. This was a baby compared to the mothers that we line catch there, but it was very exciting. My immediate thought was of fried fish and rice, the next was fried fish, rice, lemon and chilli. Sitting on a beach on a tropical island, sun setting, fish on a barbecue . . . that was my basic idea for the dish, but I also wanted to give it strong, accessible flavours: ginger, garlic, coriander, mint, lemon. This is a dish to eat on a beach without cutlery, using fingers, family around, making as much mess as possible.'

Method

1   Using a sharp knife, score the fish three times on each side.

2   Place the flour on a large plate. Season with salt and pepper. Dust fish liberally with flour inside and out.

3   Place toothpicks in gut cavity to hold gut flaps open. This will allow the fish to 'swim' upright once cooked.

4   Heat the oil in a large frying pan until very hot. The oil is hot enough when a cube of bread cooks to golden. Cook the fish, basting tail, fins, head and inside of gut throughout, until golden and crisp. Drain, upright, on absorbent paper.

5   Place the ginger, garlic, onion and chilli in a small heatproof bowl.

6   Heat the extra vegetable oil in a small saucepan until smoking. Pour over vegetables.

7   To serve, remove the toothpicks from the fish. Stand on a serving plate. Arrange the vegetable mixture around the fish. Drizzle with sesame oil. Garnish with coriander and mint. Serve with soy sauce and lemon.

Note This fish would go well with steamed rice. A small dish of lemon juice, pepper and salt combined to taste, or a dipping sauce of soy with sliced chilli and coriander leaves and very thin slices of lemon, would make a good accompaniment.

# Justine's whole salmon with fennel and chestnuts

Justine says: 'This dish was created for the MasterChef Christmas challenge that Julie and I won. When the core ingredient was revealed I knew straight away that I wanted to keep the salmon whole. There is nothing better then seeing an entire cooked fish coming to the table. The theatre of presenting and serving the whole fish is festive and enticing. Cooking a whole fish can be daunting, but certain signs tell you when it is ready – the cheeks come easily off the bone and the eyes turn white. If you're unsure, insert a skewer at the thickest end. If the liquid runs clear, it is ready.

## Method

1. Preheat the oven to 180°C (160° fan-forced).

2. Lightly grease a large piece of foil and line with baking paper. Place the salmon on top of the foil and stuff it with tarragon, fennel, garlic and eschalots. Sprinkle the lemon zest and juice over the top, dot with butter and pour over the wine. Season with salt and pepper and drizzle with oil. Fold over the foil and seal the edges. Place on an oven tray. Bake for 1 hour 20 mins or until cooked to your liking. Reserve pan juices.

3. To make the cream sauce, heat an oiled saucepan over a medium heat and cook the eschalots, stirring, until soft. Add the wine, season with salt and pepper and simmer until reduced by half. Add ⅔ cup (160 ml) pan juices from the cooking fish; reduce for another 2–4 mins. Add cream and tarragon and simmer until reduced to a thick, rich consistency, adjust with lemon juice to taste and season with salt.

4. To make the braised fennel, heat an oiled frying pan over a medium heat and cook the garlic and eschalots for 1 min. Add the fennel and cook for 4–6 mins, turning occasionally until tender and slightly caramelised. Add the lemon juice and wine, then reduce again. Add the fennel fronds and chestnuts. Cook, stirring, until hot. Season with salt and pepper.

5. Plate the fish and serve with the braised fennel, with the cream sauce in a jug to the side.

Serves 4
Preparation time: 30 mins
Cooking time: 1 hour 20 mins

1 whole salmon (2.5 kg), cleaned
1 bunch tarragon, chopped
2 fennel bulbs, sliced
2 garlic cloves, sliced
2 eschalots, sliced
zest and juice of 1 lemon
40 g butter, diced
½ cup (125 ml) white wine
2 tbs olive oil

Cream sauce
2 eschalots, finely diced
¼ cup (60 ml) white wine
½ cup (125 ml) cream
½ bunch tarragon, finely chopped

Braised fennel
2 garlic cloves, finely sliced
2 eschalots, finely sliced
2 fennel bulbs, quartered, fronds reserved
juice of ½ lemon
¼ cup (60 ml) white wine
2 cups fresh whole chestnuts, roasted and peeled (if unavailable, use canned chestnuts, drained and rinsed)

# Manu Feildel's boudin of whiting on a bed of baby spinach and beurre blanc

Serves 4
Preparation time: 40 mins
Cooking time: 10–12 mins

1 large tomato
2 tbs olive oil
8 whiting fillets (360 g),
  pin-boned and trimmed
40 g butter
200 g baby spinach
beurre blanc sauce, to serve
  (see page 29)
fish roe and parsley leaves,
  to garnish

Boudin
125 g whiting fillets, skin off
40 g eggwhites (see note)
¾ cup (180 ml) pouring cream

Manu Feildel was once head chef at Bilson's Restaurant, and is now co-owner and chef de cuisine at L'étoile. Sam was pitted against him in the very first celebrity chef challenge. They would both be cooking one of Manu's signature dishes – boudin of whiting with baby spinach and beurre blanc.

When he saw the dish, Sam looked alarmed. 'It looks like art on a plate,' he said. 'I don't stand a snowflake's chance in hell.' Manu explained that the boudin – a soft fish sausage – would be the real challenge. 'If it doesn't work, it doesn't look like a sausage. It just looks like a mess.' 'Time to cook for your life,' Gary told Sam.

Sam successfully pin boned and skinned his whiting fillet and twirled it triumphantly in the air as the other contestants cheered, but when Manu started cooking 'it was just like poetry in motion', as Julie said, and the celebrity chef had soon caught up to the amateur.

Sadly for Sam, he didn't do well enough to receive a pass through to the finals. He was proud of himself, though, and actually admitted: 'If I'd won, I wouldn't know what to do with myself.'

# Manu Feildel's boudin of whiting on a bed of baby spinach and beurre blanc

Method

1   Blanch the tomato in a saucepan of boiling water for 10–20 seconds. Transfer to a bowl of iced water and cool slightly. Peel, quarter, remove the seeds and finely dice.

2   To make the boudin, process the whiting and eggwhites in a food processor to make a smooth paste. Add the cream. Process for a few seconds until just combined and thickened slightly. Season with salt. The salt will also firm up the mixture.

3   Place a quarter of the mixture onto a piece of cling film, roll into a neat sausage shape about 3 cm diameter, and tie a knot at each end. Repeat to make 4 sausages.

4   Poach the boudin for about 7–9 mins in a large saucepan of barely simmering water until just firm to touch.

5   Heat the oil in a frying pan and add the whiting fillets, skin side down. Cook for about 2 mins, pressing with a metal spatula to maximise the contact between the skin and the pan. Turn the fish and add the butter to the pan. Cook for another minute, spooning the melted butter over as it cooks. Blanch the spinach in a saucepan of boiling water and drain well.

6   Garnish boudin with fish roe. Serve on a bed of baby spinach with beurre blanc sauce and whiting fillets. Garnish with diced tomato and parsley leaves.

Note You will need the white of a jumbo egg (67 g). If you have smaller eggs, separate the whites and lightly beat them with a fork to loosen. Weigh, and discard excess eggwhite.

# Meat

Sausages, steak, suckling pigs and so on

# How to make sausages

**1**

Tie a knot at the end of the sausage casing. Casings are slippery and can be hard to handle – it may take some getting used to.

**2**

Put the casing over the nozzle.

**3**

Bunch all of the casing up over the nozzle, like pulling a stocking up over your foot, leaving just a little bit hanging over the end.

4

Start pushing the meat through the funnel. Use the tool that comes with your sausage maker – not your fingers!

5

Use your thumb and forefinger to maintain an even pressure as the casing fills with sausage meat.

6

Twist or tie the casing to create individual sausages.

# Spicy lamb sausages

Makes 20
Preparation time: 40 mins +
   overnight refrigeration
Cooking time: 10–15 mins

1 kg boneless lamb shoulder
3 tsp cumin seeds
1 tsp ground cinnamon
1 tsp ground cardamom
1 tsp chilli flakes
1 tsp ground paprika
50 g copha
4 garlic cloves
1 tbs orange juice
1 cup (40 g) fresh breadcrumbs
natural sausage casing

'A sausage is all about simplicity.
It's not about being ridiculous,
quirky and eccentric. It's about
having lots of flavour, and above
all, it not being dry.' – George

'Stick some mincemeat inside
a bloody intestine – it can't be
that hard, can it?' – Sam

When the contestants lifted the lids of their mystery boxes one morning, they were mystified. 'There's a little bowl of intestines,' said Justine. 'And this piece of machinery.' 'You're making sausages,' Gary told them. 'What a fantastic surprise!'

They had a whole range of ingredients to choose from. Julie went for lamb with pine nuts, fetta, rosemary, lemon, garlic and onion, while Chris chose a duck and pork belly boerewors. Justine attempted a rustic Lyonnaise-style sausage, and Sam and Andre both decided on a chipolata. Poh's sausage, a kind of hybrid lap cheong, would prove to be the winner. '*That* is a sausage!' Matt said, pronouncing it 'juicy, meaty, honey sweet and delicious to eat'.

As Gary told the contestants, 'Your brain should be flooding with ideas now. If it's not, you're in trouble.' George had some final words of advice: 'Be careful your sausages don't explode in the pan! If your flame is too hot, they'll burst.'

Here's a simple recipe to get you started. Once you've mastered the basics, you can experiment and create your own designer sausage.

Method

1   Using the mincer attachment on your sausage maker, mince the lamb shoulder.

2   Dry-fry spices until fragrant. Pound with a pestle and mortar to a fine powder. Add the copha, garlic and juice. Pound to a smooth paste.

3   Using your hands, mix the lamb and breadcrumbs in a large bowl until well combined. Add the spice paste. Mix well to combine.

4   Run cold water through the sausage casing three times to clean it. Cut a length of wet casing and slide it onto the nozzle of a sausage maker, leaving a little untied casing hanging off the end. Feed the lamb through the machine, sliding the casing off the nozzle as the mince comes out. Run your hands over the sausage to expel the excess air. Tie one end in a knot, then twist the casing at even intervals to make 20 sausages. Refrigerate the sausages overnight.

5   Cook sausages in a lightly oiled frying pan until browned all over and cooked through.

# Justine's lamb roulade with spinach and mint puree

Justine says: 'This lamb roulade was an English-inspired dish, with a French twist, of course! When I was doing the invention test we had to use the leg of lamb; however, if I was doing this at home, I would ask my butcher to butterfly some lamb fillets or even better, lamb loin. Like many of the invention tests we did on MasterChef, this was one of those dishes where I had to think on the spot and come up with something that was creative, not too pedestrian (as Matt Preston would say!) and, above all, delicious. I'm passionate about this recipe because the flavours match so well. If you present this to your family and friends, I can assure you they'll be extremely impressed!'

## Method

1 Preheat oven to 180°C (160° fan-forced).

2 Finely chop 2 cloves of garlic and reserve. Place remaining bulb of garlic on oven tray and drizzle with 1 tbs olive oil. Cook in oven for 30 mins.

3 Process mushroom in a food processor until finely diced. Heat 2 tsp of the remaining oil and 20 g butter in a frying pan over high heat. Add mushroom, eschalot and half of the reserved chopped garlic. Cook, stirring, until mushroom is soft. Season with salt and pepper. Stir in 1 tbs parsley. Set aside to cool.

4 In a small saucepan of boiling water, blanch spinach and mint for 30–40 seconds or until spinach has just wilted. Drain and place in iced water to cool.

5 Drain spinach mixture, squeezing out excess water. Blend in a blender with cream, 2 cloves of the roasted garlic and 20 g of the remaining butter until smooth.

6 Place potatoes in a saucepan of cold water. Bring to the boil. Cook until tender, then drain. Cool slightly, peel and chop coarsely.

7 Pound lamb with a meat mallet until it is 5 mm thick.

8 Combine extra cream with mustard in a small bowl. Spread a thin layer of mustard cream on top of the lamb and top with the mushroom mixture, then roll tightly from the long side and tie with kitchen string at 3 cm intervals.

9 Heat 1 tbs of the remaining oil in a frying pan over high heat. Add lamb. Cook, turning until browned evenly on all sides. Place in the oven for a further 15 mins or until cooked to your liking. Remove and allow to rest, covered, for 10 mins. Remove string, slice thickly.

10 Heat remaining oil and butter in a frying pan over high heat. Add potatoes, cook 6–8 mins or until crisp. Add remaining garlic and parsley, cook for a further 2 mins, season with salt and pepper.

11 Spoon the spinach and mint puree onto a serving plate, top with lamb, and place potatoes on the side.

Serves 2
Preparation time: 30 mins +
  1 hour refrigeration
Cooking time: about 30 mins

1 bulb garlic
¼ cup (60 ml) olive oil
1 large field mushroom, roughly chopped
50 g butter
1 eschalot, finely diced
2 tbs roughly chopped parsley
1 bunch English spinach, leaves only
¼ cup mint leaves
½ cup pure cream
5 small kipfler potatoes, washed
600 g lamb loin, butterflied
2 tsp pure cream, extra
1 tsp hot English mustard

# Adrian Richardson's stuffed loin of lamb with pommes galette

In the final celebrity chef challenge, Julie went up against Adrian Richardson, head chef and owner of Melbourne's La Luna bistro. Adrian's chosen dish was a stuffed loin of lamb with pommes galette and a beetroot glaze. Julie had a 10-minute head start and needed every minute of it – her first task was to debone the lamb. She burnt herself badly along the way, but was soon back in control, and as the clock ticked down the last 5 minutes she was calmly plating up, looking like a real contender. The judges were full of praise for her efforts, but she was no match for the man Gary called the 'king of butchers', who received three near-perfect scores of 9 out of 10.

Serves 4
Preparation time: 1½ hours
Cooking time: 30 mins

Lamb saddle
1 lamb saddle, loin, fillet and
  flank attached
2 tbs unsalted butter
2 eschalots, finely diced
2 garlic cloves, crushed
400 g baby spinach
½ bunch fresh thyme, leaves
  chopped
¼ bunch fresh rosemary, leaves
  chopped
200 ml extra-virgin olive oil

Pommes galette
2 large nicola potatoes, peeled
100 g unsalted butter, melted

Beetroot glaze
¼ cup (50 g) brown sugar
¼ cup (60 ml) port
2 tbs sherry vinegar
100 g beetroot, diced or grated

1 tbs extra-virgin olive oil
baby celery leaves, to garnish
2 tsp chives, finely chopped

Method

1    To make the stuffed lamb saddle, preheat the oven to 190°C (170°
     fan-forced). Cut the fillet and loin from the bone, leaving enough fat
     from the flank to wrap the loin. You should end up with two loins,
     each with a flap of fat, and 2 thin fillets.

2    Melt half the butter in a small frying pan. Sweat half the eschalot
     and garlic until soft, then add half the spinach and sauté until wilted.
     Remove from the pan and cool.

3    Lay the fillet next to the loin on the fat. Season the meat with salt
     and pepper and sprinkle with the herbs. Lay the spinach mixture
     along the loins. Roll the flank around the meat to form a log and
     tie with twine. Seal in a hot, lightly oiled ovenproof frying pan until
     browned all over. Roast in the oven for 12–15 mins, until medium
     rare. Stand the meat, covered, to rest.

4    Meanwhile, to make the pommes galette, line a baking tray with
     non-stick baking paper. Using a mandolin or a very sharp knife, cut
     the potatoes into 3 mm thick slices. Arrange the slices overlapping
     into four rounds on the prepared tray. Brush with butter and season.
     Bake for 15–20 mins, until golden brown and tender.

5    To make the beetroot glaze, cook the sugar in a small saucepan until
     melted and caramelised. Stir in the port and vinegar, then add the
     beetroot. Simmer for 10 mins, until the beetroot is tender and the
     sauce is slightly thickened.

6    To make each spinach ball, choose about 32 large leaves from
     the remaining spinach. Blanch these leaves in boiling water for
     30 seconds, then arrange them overlapping in a star shape onto
     a clean tea towel. (Make spinach balls one at a time, as you will
     need to use the tea towel to roll up each ball.) Melt the remaining
     butter in a large frying pan and sauté the remaining eschalot and
     garlic. Add the remaining spinach and cook until wilted. Season
     with salt and pepper. Cool, drain and squeeze out excess liquid,
     then roughly chop. Divide evenly between the blanched spinach
     leaves, and use the tea towel to help roll up the leaves around the
     filling to form a ball.

7    To serve, cut the meat into thick slices and arrange on the plate.
     Place the pommes galette on the plate and top with a spinach ball.
     Drizzle the meat and the plate with the beetroot glaze, olive oil and
     chopped chives. Scatter with baby celery leaves.

MasterTip
If you're not confident boning the lamb saddle, ask your butcher to
prepare the meat for you to fill and tie up. Watch how it's done, if you
can, and then have a go next time.

# Chris's steak tartare

Chris says: 'Winning the French invention test for my version of the classic steak tartare was a crucial turning point for me. Not only was it my first invention win but it gave me confidence that the type of food I love might actually find a place within the competition. It also showed that going out on a limb could pay off. Being an invention test, I still had to put a spin on this old classic. Fortunately the soy sauce I used as a replacement for the traditional Worcestershire and Tabasco worked a treat and gave it a salty depth that worked well. The key is to have the freshest beef you can find and keep it really cold at all times; cut it and put it in a bowl over ice while you mix in the other ingredients. The warmer it gets, the softer it gets and it can go mushy. You need to control the temperature closely to maintain the integrity of the meat. When I plated up for the judges and George announced that he didn't like raw meat, once again I thought I was history. Fortunately he gave it a go, liked it and I scored the win. Phew!'

Serves 2
Preparation time: 15 mins
Cooking time: nil

400 g rib eye beef, chilled
6 cornichons, finely diced
4 eschalots, finely diced
2 tsp Dijon mustard, plus extra
  to serve
2 tsp soy sauce
2 slices brioche
2 egg yolks
salt flakes, to serve

Method

1   Using a very sharp knife, finely dice the beef. Combine the beef, cornichons, eschalots, Dijon and soy in a bowl. Adjust the Dijon and soy to taste. Keep cold in the fridge.

2   Heat an oiled frying pan over a medium heat and pan-fry the brioche until golden on both sides.

3   Place a 9 cm ring mould on each serving plate and spoon the beef mixture into the mould. Make a small indentation in the top and gently pour in the egg yolk.

4   Carefully remove the ring mould. Place a teaspoon of salt flakes and a teaspoon of Dijon to the side of the plate with the toasted brioche and serve immediately.

# Julie's steak with tarragon salt

Julie says: 'I remember as one of my favourite moments in the MasterChef competition the judges getting excited about this dish. They loved the trussing of the steak, and also the unusual tarragon salt. I learned from a friend about rosemary salt, which goes beautifully with lamb dishes. I have since made a number of flavoured salts – it's fun to play around and see what works. Herbs, zests, spices, seeds – these things give a great lift to the flavour of a dish.'

Serves 2
Preparation time: 30 mins
Cooking time: 30 mins

2 potatoes, peeled
2 tbs duck fat
2 tsp olive oil
400 g rib eye steak
60 g butter
1 garlic clove, finely diced
4 medium mushrooms (150 g),
  stalks removed, finely sliced
2 tbs brandy
1 cup (250 ml) veal glaze
1 tbs cream
50 g green beans

Tarragon salt
1 tsp rock salt
½ tsp tarragon

Method

1   Cut each potato into six chips.

2   Heat the duck fat in a frying pan over medium heat. Add the potatoes. Cook, turning occasionally, until browned and tender.

3   Cut an incision between the bone and the steak and tie with cooking string, to help retain shape. Heat oil and butter in a frying pan over a high heat and cook the steak for 3–4 minutes each side for medium or until cooked to your liking. Spoon over the butter and oil while cooking.

4   Melt the butter in a frying pan over medium heat. Add the garlic and the mushrooms. Cook, stirring, until soft. Add the brandy and allow the alcohol to cook out for 1 min. Add the veal glaze, simmer for 2–3 mins, then strain the mixture. Reserve the mushrooms.

5   Pour the sauce into a clean frying pan and simmer until reduced slightly. Stir in the cream and reserved mushrooms.

6   Bring a saucepan of salted water to the boil, reduce to a simmer and blanch the beans for 2–3 mins.

7   To make the tarragon salt, pound the rock salt and tarragon leaves using a pestle and mortar.

8   Serve the steak, chips and beans with the mushroom sauce and tarragon salt.

# Aaron's beef pithivier

Aaron says: 'I made this dish in the French invention test and it was my proudest moment on the show. The TV ads leading up to the screening of that episode made a big deal of it, with tag lines such as "Mr Molecular Gastronomy takes a huge risk . . . Can he pull it off?" But although it might sound complicated, it's a really simple dish.'

When Aaron cooked this dish, George said he was really proud of him for going out on a limb. He told him: 'What I really like about it is the pastry. It's actually really crumbly and salty, and it's weirdly nice.' Aaron was chuffed, saying: 'Weird is good. Nice is even better.'

## Method

1. To make the pithivier, preheat oven to 180°C (160°C fan-forced). Heat the oil in a large saucepan, and cook 350 g of the beef with most of the onion and garlic (reserve about 2 tbs onion and ½ tsp garlic for the jus) until brown. Season with salt. Add the veal stock, carrot, leek, celery and thyme. Bring to the boil. Reduce heat and simmer, uncovered, for about 1 hour, or until the meat is tender and the mixture has thickened. Cool completely.

2. Cut four 8 cm rounds and four 6 cm rounds from the pastry. Place the smaller circles on a baking tray lined with non-stick baking paper, and brush the edge with egg wash. Mound the filling in the centre, leaving a 3 cm border around the edge. Cover with the larger circle and lightly press down the edges. Brush the top with egg wash. Refrigerate for at least 30 mins before decorating.

3. Using the dull edge of a paring knife or a spatula, press it against the sides of the pithivier to seal. Decorate the top by lightly scoring the pastry, from the centre, moving towards the edge in half circles, leaving 1 cm spaces between the cuts. Return to the fridge until ready to bake.

4. To make the pomme puree, preheat the oven to 200°C (180°C fan-forced). Roast the potatoes on a bed of rock salt until tender when pierced with a knife or skewer. Cool slightly. Remove skin. Press the flesh through a drum sieve while still hot (using a pastry scrape works best). Add butter and milk. Mash until smooth.

5. For the mushroom duxelle, heat 1tbs truffle oil in a frying pan, add the mushrooms and sauté until lightly coloured. Add the butter and allow to foam, then add the sliced garlic and a sprig of thyme. Cook until the mushrooms are golden brown, then remove from the heat and strain the mix into a colander to remove any excess butter and oil. Place mushrooms on a chopping board, pick out the garlic and thyme and chop the mushrooms. Set aside in a small saucepan.

6. For the veal jus, heat the oil in a small saucepan and cook the remaining 50 g beef with the thyme and the reserved garlic and onion. Season with salt. Once well caramelised, deglaze the pan with the stock. Add the star-anise. Cook until reduced by half. Strain the mix through a fine sieve twice and set aside.

7. Preheat the oven to 180°C (160°C fan-forced). Bake the pithivier for 25 mins or until the pastry is puffed and golden brown. To finish the veal jus, bring to the boil and remove from the heat. Whisk in the butter a little at a time to thicken. Gently reheat the pomme puree and mushroom duxelle, and serve.

Serves 4
Preparation time: 30 mins
Cooking time: 1 hour 25 mins

### Pithivier

2 tbs olive oil
400 g beef (scotch fillet or rib eye), cut into 1 cm dice
1 small onion, diced
2 garlic cloves, thinly sliced
2 cups (500 ml) salt-reduced veal stock
1 small carrot, peeled and thinly sliced
1 leek, trimmed and thinly sliced
1½ sticks celery, peeled and thinly sliced
2 sprigs thyme
2 sheets frozen puff pastry, thawed
2 eggs, lightly beaten

### Pomme puree

6 washed potatoes (about 600 g)
30 g unsalted butter
1/3 cup (80 ml) milk

### Mushroom duxelle

1 tbs white truffle oil
200 g button mushrooms
250 g butter, diced
50 g king brown mushrooms
1 garlic clove, thinly sliced
1 sprig thyme

### Veal jus

1 tbs oil
1 sprig thyme
¾ cup (180 ml) salt-reduced veal stock
2 star-anise
10 g cold diced unsalted butter

# Brent's braised rabbit in a capsicum, tomato and fennel sauce

Brent says: 'I had just banged out a feed for an army in only an hour, with just 60 seconds in the pantry to prepare. I'd done rabbit and several side dishes of Italian vegetables. With 4 plates of food on the cold steel counter in front of me, this could have gone horribly wrong. I was quietly preparing myself for the worst when George rocked forward on his toes, slapped his hands and said, "Yeah!" I wish I could have hit the pause button on this moment so I could soak George's words in for just a little longer. "Brent, you have captured the Italian spirit of generosity."

'Bugger! I bit my knuckle a bit too hard with shock. Apart from my very first tap on the tasting bench from Matt, back in the Top Fifty (not for my pork alla butane), this was the best comment I'd received so far.'

Serves 2
Preparation time: 20 mins
Cooking time: about 35 mins

2 tbs olive oil
2 rabbit legs
½ red onion, sliced
1 fennel bulb, sliced,
  tops reserved
1 red capsicum, sliced
400 g can diced tomatoes
2 garlic cloves (leave whole)
1 cup (250 ml) white wine
2 tbs finely chopped flat-leaf
  parsley, reserve stalks
quartered green olives,
  to serve

## Method

1   Preheat the oven to 180°C (160° fan-forced). Heat the oil in a deep frying pan over high heat. Cook the rabbit legs until lightly browned and set aside. Sauté the onion until soft and season to taste.

2   Add the fennel, capsicum, tomatoes, garlic and wine. Stir to combine. Return the rabbit to the pan. Sprinkle with reserved fennel tops and parsley stalks. Simmer, covered, over medium heat for 10 mins, or until the rabbit is tender.

3   Discard the fennel and parsley stalks from the sauce. Remove the rabbit and place on an oven tray. Roast for 8–10 mins.

4   Cook the sauce, uncovered, for about 5 mins, or until reduced slightly. Season to taste. Plate the rabbit and spoon over the sauce. Sprinkle with parsley and green olives to serve.

# Ben O'Donoghue's seared kangaroo with creamed corn

Serves 4
Preparation time: 30 mins
Cooking time: about 30 mins

4 kangaroo fillets
2 tbs thyme leaves, roughly
  chopped
freshly ground black pepper
25 g dried porcini mushrooms
25 g dried morel mushrooms
2 cups (280 g) fresh corn kernels
2 cups (500 ml) cream
2 garlic cloves, thinly sliced
1 large eschalot, roughly
  chopped
1 cup (250 ml) cabernet
  sauvignon
1 cup (250 ml) veal jus
100 g butter, diced
2 king brown mushrooms,
  thinly sliced
50 g shiitake mushrooms, sliced
1 tbs chopped flat-leaf parsley
1 lemon, halved
fresh truffle, thinly sliced, or
  truffle oil (optional)
½ cup (125 ml) port
parsely, to garnish

Lucas cooked off against well-known chef, author and TV presenter Ben O'Donoghue in the celebrity chef challenge. At stake was a chance to skip straight through to the final week of MasterChef. When Ben revealed his dish – seared kangaroo loin and creamed corn with a red wine reduction and wild mushrooms – Lucas looked apprehensive, telling George he'd never cooked with kangaroo before.

Lucas was given a 15-minute head start on Ben, who coached him in a new technique, sous vide – cooking meat at a low temperature in a vacuum pack. When Ben got his own dish underway, he caught up to Lucas in no time. As Julie observed, he was 'like some kind of cooking machine. He just got started and wham! wham! wham!'

When Ben had everything under control, he went round to help Lucas, telling him it was time to take his kangaroo out of the pot. With 5 minutes to go, Ben started plating up while Lucas raced to finish, getting his food on the plate only at the very last second.

In a surprise upset, George and Gary scored Lucas's dish slightly higher than Ben's, sending him leapfrogging through to the finals. As Lucas hugged the other contestants goodbye the expression on his face made it clear he couldn't quite believe his luck.

# Ben O'Donoghue's seared kangaroo with creamed corn

Method

1   Season the kangaroo with the chopped thyme, salt and freshly ground black pepper, then allow to infuse for 10 mins. Soak the dried mushrooms in ½ cup boiling water until softened.

2   Place the corn and cream into a saucepan with half the garlic. Cover with a round of baking paper and cook until the corn is tender and the cream has reduced by half. Puree with a stick blender until very smooth and season to taste.

3   Meanwhile, combine the eschalot and red wine in a saucepan and bring to the boil. Reduce the heat slightly and simmer until reduced to a syrup. Add the veal jus and cook until reduced by three-quarters. Remove from the heat. Stir in 30 g of the butter and keep warm.

4   Heat 30 g of the remaining butter in a saucepan and add the king brown mushrooms. Sauté for 1–2 mins. Drain the soaked mushrooms, reserving the liquid. Add the drained mushrooms and sauté for 2–3 mins. Add the reserved liquid and cook down until it is almost evaporated. Add the shiitake mushrooms and cook for 2 mins. Stir in the parsley and a squeeze of lemon juice and season to taste.

5   Place the kangaroo fillets into vacuum bags and divide 20 g butter and the truffle (or a drizzle of truffle oil) between the bags. Add ¼ cup of port to each bag and seal. These can be kept at room temp around 30 mins or until required. Heat a large pot of water to 70°C and poach each kangaroo fillet for 10 mins. Remove kangaroo from bag.

6   Melt the remaining butter in a frying pan until foaming, add the kangaroo and sear all over. Transfer to a plate to rest. Add the remaining garlic and a little more truffle (or a drizzle of truffle oil) to the butter. Spoon this over the kangaroo and allow to infuse.

7   Serve the kangaroo over braised mushrooms and creamed corn. Drizzle with the sauce and garnish with parsley.

---

MasterTip

Ben says that the crucial thing with this dish is not to overcook the meat. You can go under, but never go over.

# Julia's goat, spinach and fetta pie

Julia says: 'Of the dishes I cooked in the competition, this one most closely represents the kind of food I love to cook. I told myself from the beginning that if I was ever faced with goat in an invention test, I would have to choose it. When the opportunity arose, I couldn't resist! Goat is one of my favourite meats; usually I use the shoulder or leg as these yield the tenderest meat after long, slow cooking. This was one of the easiest dishes to come up with. I just thought of all those flavours that represent Greece to me – sour lemons, creamy fetta, fresh spinach, crisp filo pastry, aniseed from ouzo and a bright splash of sweet beetroot. Just don't burn the pie!'

Method

1. Preheat oven to 180ºC (160° fan-forced). To prepare the filling, heat half the olive oil in a frying pan over medium-high heat. Cook goat until browned all over, then remove from pan and set aside. Heat remaining oil in pan and sauté onion until soft. Return goat to pan, add ouzo and allow to cook down for 3–5 mins. Add chicken stock, lemon zest, juice and oregano. Reduce heat and simmer, stirring occasionally, for at least an hour or until very tender.

2. To prepare the beetroot, bring a saucepan of water to the boil and add the unpeeled beetroot. Simmer, covered, for 30–40 mins or until very tender. Cool, then peel. Dice 1½ beetroot into small even cubes. Combine the red wine vinegar, ouzo and lemon zest in a small saucepan and bring to the boil. Add diced beetroot and simmer for 6 mins. Place water, oil, fetta and remaining beetroot in a mini food processor. Process until smooth. Season to taste.

3. To prepare the spinach, heat the oil in a frying pan over medium heat. Sauté leek and garlic until soft. Season with salt and pepper. Add spinach and lemon juice. Stir until spinach wilts. Drain spinach through a sieve, using back of spoon to press and remove all liquid. Drain on absorbent paper. Chop coarsely. Combine spinach and fetta in a small bowl.

4. Strain goat mixture through a sieve, reserving cooking liquid. Discard lemon zest and oregano. Mix goat with spinach mixture, add a little of the strained goat juices to moisten, and adjust seasoning.

5. Layer 4 sheets of filo on the workbench, brushing with butter or oil in between each layer. Grease a 10 cm loose-based tart tin and place the filo into the tin, with the excess hanging over the edge. Spoon a quarter of the filling into the centre of the tart and fold the overhanging pastry in toward the centre. Repeat with the remaining pastry and filling to make 4 tarts. Bake for 10–15 mins, until crisp and golden.

6. To serve, smear beetroot puree across the plate and spoon pickled beetroot to one side. Place the pie in the centre and scatter the walnuts and broad beans around the plate. Top with dill.

Serves 4
Preparation time: 30 mins
Cooking time: 1 hour 20 mins

16 sheets filo pastry
olive oil or melted butter to brush pastry
40 g walnuts, toasted
100 g broad beans, podded, blanched and peeled
dill

Filling
⅓ cup (60 ml) olive oil
1 boned goat shoulder, fat and sinew removed, very finely diced or minced
1 onion, finely diced
½ cup (125 ml) ouzo
½ cup (125 ml) chicken stock
2 cm wide strip of lemon zest
2 tbs lemon juice
1 tsp fresh oregano leaves

Beetroot
3 medium beetroot
¼ cup (60 ml) red wine vinegar
¼ cup (60 ml) ouzo
2 cm wide strip of lemon zest
2 tbs water
2 tbs olive oil
80 g fetta, crumbled

Spinach
2 tbs olive oil
1 leek, finely diced
1 garlic clove, crushed
100 g baby spinach, rinsed
½ lemon, juiced
100 g fetta, crumbled

# Hong Kong suckling pig

'This isn't wind – this is dragon's breath. We stand on the brow of the great dragon who winds his way here from mainland China, and whose head is here amongst these mountains. Today we are pirate kings and you are our pirates. We're sending you out, down there into the dragon's den. You have your map, you have your recipes, you have your money, you have but three and a half hours to get this challenge completed! Your time starts . . . NOW!' So said Matt Preston, the world's greatest food critic, bellowing above a howling gale and looking out over Hong Kong from on high.

Invention test winner Chris chose the pairs for the Hong Kong super challenge: André and Sam versus Justine and Julie. The four contestants were summoned to the top of Hong Kong's highest peak, where the judges gave them a map and HK$1000 and told them to find their own way back to their hotel – buying ingredients for a three-course meal along the way. They had precious little time to complete the challenge, and on their shopping list was a suckling pig.

Back at their hotel, the four contestants had access to a fully kitted-out commercial kitchen – a definite advantage – but the recipe overleaf is one you can prepare in your own home. Careful planning is still called for, though – you'll need to order your pig from the butcher at least a week in advance.

# Hong Kong suckling pig

Serves 8–10
Preparation time: 30 mins +
  2 hours refrigeration +
  20 mins resting
Cooking time: 3 hours 15 mins

1 suckling pig (approx 8 kg)
2 tbs sea salt
1½ tbs Chinese five-spice
2 tbs malt syrup
1 cup (250 ml) soy sauce

Sauce
2 tbs hoisin
2 tbs char sui
1 tbs sesame oil
1 tsp red wine vinegar
1 tbs shaoxing wine

Top right
Sam and André's pig
Bottom right
Justine and Julie's pig
Bottom left
The Hong Kong pirate kings

Method

1  Rub the pig thoroughly with the salt inside and out and leave to season, refrigerated, for 2 hours.

2  Bring a large saucepan of water to the boil. Place the pig in the sink. Tip boiling water over the pig and into the cavity to rinse off the salt. Wipe and dry thoroughly with absorbent paper.

3  Preheat oven to 200°C (180° fan-forced).

4  Combine the five-spice, malt syrup and soy in a medium jug. Pour over pig and rub evenly over the skin and onto the flesh in the cavity.

5  Place the suckling pig onto a wire rack over a large baking dish. Roast for 15 mins. Reduce the oven to 140°C (120° fan-forced) and cook for a further 3 hours. Remove from the oven and rest for 15–20 mins before carving.

6  To make the sauce, combine all the ingredients in a small bowl. Serve with the carved pig.

---

MasterTip
You don't want your pig to have leathery skin, so even when the meat is resting, don't cover it up. As Matt says: 'Steam is the enemy of crackle.'

# Chris's roast half pig head

Serves 2
Preparation time: 15 mins
Cooking time: 3 hours 10 mins

1 generous tbs duck fat
10 whole eschalots, peeled
10 garlic cloves, peeled
1 bouquet garni (thyme,
  rosemary, parsley and bay
  leaves)
½ pig's head
1½ cups (375 ml) good white
  wine
½ cup (125 ml) brandy
4 cups (1 litre) good chicken
  stock
2 tsp Dijon mustard
1 bunch English spinach
1 bunch watercress, picked
  into sprigs

Chris says: 'Cooking this dish has to be my absolute highlight from MasterChef. However, while I was cooking it my inner voice was questioning my sanity for producing a dish that would be very visually confronting for many people. This is an adaptation of a recipe from a true master chef, Fergus Henderson from St John's in London. I have not always been this offal-eating madman that I am now perceived to be, and it is chefs like Fergus who have encouraged me to open my mind and tastebuds and to try new, different and ultimately delicious things. When I cooked this dish, I did not realise nor was I prepared for the huge response I would get from people who love to cook like this or wanted to try it out. There is obviously an underground movement out there of Pig Head lovers and I have been more than happy to join the fold. My fears that the judges would crucify me abated when I cracked the skin with an audible crunch and their eyes lit up. I can't explain the sense of relief and the joy I felt when they liked the dish. It is something I will never forget. Go the Pig Head!'

## Method

1   Preheat the oven to 180°C (160° fan forced). Melt the duck fat in a flameproof, ovenproof dish large enough to fit the pig's head. Add the eschalots and garlic. Cook, stirring, until browned. Add the bouquet garni to the middle of the pan and place the pig's head over the top of the ingredients in the pan.

2   Pour over the wine, brandy and enough stock to bring the liquid level halfway up the side of the dish. Season with salt and pepper. Cover with non-stick baking paper and then foil, to keep the baking paper in place.

3   Roast for 2½ hours. Remove the paper and roast for a further 30 mins. The skin should be beautiful and crisp, and the meat and fat meltingly tender when done.

4   Remove the head from the dish. Place the dish on the stovetop and stir in the mustard. Add the spinach and watercress and stir until wilted. Serve the head on a bed of the wilted greens. Enjoy with a glass of beer and good company!

# Desserts

Sweet treats: from scones and jam to tarte tatin

# Simple pastry cream

Makes about 1 cup (250 ml)
Preparation time: 5 mins
Cooking time: about 5 mins +
  cooling

200 ml milk
½ vanilla bean, split
3 egg yolks
¼ cup (55 g) caster sugar
1 tbs cornflour
20 g butter

Pastry cream is used to fill profiteroles, eclairs and other pastry goodies. This recipe makes 1 cup, enough to fill a 22 cm pastry shell. Double the quantity and you'll have enough to fill a batch of eclairs or profiteroles (see page 196 for a recipe for choux pastry).

Method

1   Stir the milk and vanilla bean in a small saucepan over medium heat until almost boiling. Remove bean.

2   Meanwhile, whisk the yolks, sugar and cornflour in a bowl until thick and pale. Gradually whisk the hot milk into the egg mixture. Return the mixture to a clean saucepan. Whisk over a medium heat until the custard boils and thickens. Spread over a tray to cool rapidly. Cover the surface of the custard with cling film to prevent a skin forming.

3   When the mixture has cooled to 55°C, transfer it to a bowl and stir through the butter. Refrigerate to cool completely.

# Adriano Zumbo's crème pâtissière

Makes about 1.5 litres
Preparation time: 10 mins
Cooking time: about 5 mins +
  cooling

1.3 litres milk
2 vanilla beans, split
18 egg yolks (330 g)
330 g caster sugar
130 g cornflour
130 g butter

Crème pâtissière is just the French name for pastry cream. If you're going to attempt Adriano Zumbo's crazy croquembouche, you'll need lots of it. This recipe makes enough to fill about 100 profiteroles.

Method

1   Stir the milk and vanilla beans in a large saucepan over medium heat until almost boiling. Remove beans.

2   Meanwhile, whisk the yolks, sugar and cornflour in a bowl until thick and pale. Gradually whisk the hot milk into the egg mixture. Return the mixture to a clean saucepan. Whisk over a medium heat until the custard boils and thickens. Spread over a tray to cool rapidly. Cover the surface of the custard with cling film to prevent a skin forming.

3   When the mixture has cooled to 55°C, transfer it to a bowl and stir through the butter. Refrigerate to cool completely.

# Matt Moran's caramel sauce

You'll need this caramel sauce to make Matt Moran's warm pear tart (page 212) – the one Justine made when she cooked off against him in the celebrity chef challenge.

Makes 1¾ cups (435 ml)
Preparation time: 10 mins
Cooking time: 5 mins

1 cup (220 g) caster sugar
¾ cup (180 ml) cream
100 g butter, diced

## Method

1   Heat the sugar in a non-stick saucepan for 3–4 mins, until it turns a dark golden-brown colour.

2   Remove from the heat and add the cream and butter.

3   Whisk until all the ingredients have come together. Cool in the fridge.

# Classic chocolate sauce

A good, rich chocolate sauce should be part of every cook's repertoire. Pour it over cakes, tarts, crepes, stewed or poached fruits, or even over a simple bowl of ice-cream to take your desserts to the next level.

Makes about 1 cup (250 ml)
Preparation time: 10 mins
Cooking time: 3–4 mins

½ cup (125 ml) pouring cream
150 g good dark chocolate, chopped
1 tbs brown sugar
1 tsp vanilla extract

## Method

1   Heat the cream in a small saucepan until hot.

2   Add the chocolate and sugar. Stand over medium-low heat until beginning to soften. Remove from heat, then stir until combined and smooth.

3   Stir in the vanilla extract. Serve warm.

# Simple choux pastry

Makes 24 profiteroles or
  24 little eclairs
Preparation time: 20–25 mins +
  1 hour cooling
Cooking time: 15–25 mins

50 g butter, chopped
¾ cup (115 g) plain flour
3 eggs
200 g dark chocolate, melted

Choux pastry is much simpler than it looks, but you might need a
few trial runs to master it. It's worth the effort. Profiteroles filled
with pastry cream and smothered in chocolate sauce are easy (and
fun) to whip up, and they impress dinner party guests far more
than they really should. This recipe can also be used to make mini
eclairs for an elegant afternoon tea – just pipe long shapes rather
than balls.

Method

1   Preheat the oven to 210°C (190° fan-forced). Line 2 large baking
    trays with non-stick baking paper. Place the butter in a large
    saucepan and add ¾ cup (185 ml) water. Cook over medium heat
    until the butter has melted and the mixture comes to the boil. Sift
    the flour into the pan and beat with a wooden spoon over the
    heat for about 1 min, until the mixture comes away from the sides
    of the pan.

2   Transfer the mixture to a bowl and cool slightly, stirring to release the
    heat. Add the yolks one at a time, beating well with electric beaters
    between each addition, until the mixture is very thick and glossy. For
    profiteroles, drop level tablespoons of the mixture onto the trays,
    leaving 5 cm between them. To make little eclairs, spoon the mixture
    into a piping bag fitted with a round 1.5 cm nozzle, and pipe
    24 lengths of dough onto the tray, each about 8 cm long.

3   Bake for 20–25 mins (for profiteroles) or 15–18 mins (for little eclairs)
    until puffed and golden brown. Using a skewer, pierce a small hole in
    the side of each puff. Return to the oven, turn off and prop the door
    ajar. Leave to cool.

4   To fill the profiteroles, pierce a hole in the side. Fill a piping bag with
    a double quantity of simple pastry cream (see page 194). Eclairs can
    be halved horizontally and filled. Alternatively, fill with sweetened
    whipped cream. Ice with melted dark chocolate.

# Adriano Zumbo's choux pastry

To make a croquembouche, you need an industrial quantity of choux pastry. Here's Adriano Zumbo's own recipe. It makes around 100 balls – enough for a mighty tower of pastry puffs.

Makes around 100 puffs
Preparation time: 1 hour 20 mins
   + 1 hour cooling
Cooking time: 1 hour 20 mins

Method

1   Preheat the oven to 210°C (190° fan-forced). Lightly grease 4 oven trays.

2   Combine the butter, sugar, milk and salt in a large heavy-based saucepan with 425 ml water and bring to the boil. Remove from the heat and, using a wooden spoon, quickly beat in the flour. Return to the heat and continue beating until the mixture comes together and leaves the side of the pan. Keep beating over a low heat for 1–2 mins to cook the flour. Remove from the heat and cool slightly.

3   Transfer to a large bowl. Using electric beaters, beat the mixture to release any more heat. Add the eggs one at a time, beating well between each addition, until all the eggs have been added and the mixture is thick and glossy. Beat for a few more minutes, or until thickened. Pipe and bake as directed (see page 216).

400 g butter
20 g sugar
530 ml milk
20 g salt
530 g flour
16 eggs

# Sweet shortcrust pastry

Makes enough for a 22 cm
   tart tin
Preparation time: 20 mins +
   20 mins resting
Cooking time: 30 mins

1½ cups (225 g) plain flour
2 tbs icing sugar
125 g cold butter, diced
3–4 tbs iced water

Sweet shortcrust pastry is one of those classics all home cooks used to make without even consulting a cookbook. We tend to be frightened of pastry these days, but it's really not that hard. For a simple but impressive dessert, follow George and Gary's example and make a basic tart shell, then spoon in sweetened whipped cream and heap berries over it, as they did in a masterclass.

Method

1   Place the flour, icing sugar and butter into a food processor. Using the pulse button, process in short bursts until the mixture resembles breadcrumbs.

2   Add the water and process in short bursts until the dough comes together in small moist particles (pinch some with your fingers to check). If it seems dry, add a little more water.

3   Tip out onto a work surface and gather the dough together. Roll out on a sheet of non-stick baking paper, and carefully invert over a 22 cm loose-based tart tin. Peel away the paper (keep it) and gently ease the pastry into the tin. Run your rolling pin across the top to trim any overhanging pastry. Refrigerate for 20 mins.

4   Preheat the oven to 180°C (160° fan-forced). To 'blind bake', lay the paper over the pastry and fill with dried beans or pastry weights. Bake for 15 mins, then remove the paper and beans and cook for another 15 mins, or until it's lightly golden and the base is dry. Cool completely before filling.

# Scones

Makes 12
Preparation time: 15 mins
Cooking time: 12–15 mins

2½ cups (375 g) self-raising flour
30 g butter
¾ cup (185 ml) milk
extra milk, to brush over
jam and cream, to serve

Scones are the very definition of low input/high outcome. They take ten minutes to make, but when you whip up a batch out of thin air, everyone thinks you're a magician. Even plain scones with butter and jam will impress, and once you know what you're doing, you can start to experiment. In a masterclass, Gary made lemon and date scones by adding the finely grated zest of a lemon and some chopped dates to his dough. You could try adding sultanas or chopped glacé ginger after rubbing in the butter, or perhaps a pinch of mixed spice when sifting the flour. Substitute the milk with buttermilk for a slightly different result, or use cream instead of milk for a richer scone.

1  Preheat oven to 200°C (180° fan-forced). Line a large oven tray with non-stick baking paper. Sift the flour into a large bowl and add the butter. Using your fingertips, rub in the butter until evenly combined. If it seems dry, add a little water, until you have a soft dough.

2  Make a well in the centre and add the milk. Mix in with a knife until evenly moistened, then gather the dough together with your hands. Turn out onto a lightly floured surface and roll out to 2 cm thick.

3  Use a 6 cm round cutter to cut rounds from the dough, as close together as possible to get the most scones from the first rolling of dough. Gently press scraps together and lightly re-roll, then cut out more scones.

4  Place rounds, just touching each other, on the prepared oven tray. Brush the tops lightly with milk. Bake for 12–15 mins, until risen and golden brown. Transfer to a wire rack to cool slightly, then split and serve with jam and cream.

---

MasterTip

Plain flour can be used instead of self-raising if you add baking powder to the flour before sifting. One teaspoon of baking powder for every cup of flour is a good rule of thumb.

# Lemon curd

Makes 2 cups (500 ml)
Preparation time: 5 mins
Cooking time: 15 mins

3 eggs
2 egg yolks
¾ cup (165 g) caster sugar
finely grated zest of 1 lemon
juice of 3 lemons
125 g butter, chopped

In a masterclass, George and Gary made lemon curd, an old-fashioned kitchen classic, then smeared it across a wooden serving plate. Next they crumbled a batch of Julie's lemon diva cupcakes (see page 205) over the top, added quenelles of a lemony crème fraîche and finished it off with a drizzle of lemon vanilla syrup. Thinking like a chef means taking reliable old standards and presenting them in a way that makes them new again.

This basic recipe makes a light, sweet, golden curd, like sunshine in a jar. You'll want to eat it by the spoonful.

Method

1   Whisk the eggs, egg yolks and sugar in a bowl until the mixture is well combined and the sugar has dissolved. Whisk in the zest and juice.

2   Place the bowl over a pan of simmering water. Don't let the bottom of the bowl touch the water. Cook, stirring regularly, for 15 mins, until thickened – the mixture should coat the back of a spoon.

3   Add the butter gradually during cooking, and whisk until combined before adding more.

4   Cool and spoon into a wide-mouthed jar.

MasterTip
For a delicious twist, replace the lemon zest and juice with ¾ cup passionfruit pulp.

# Julie's lemon diva cupcakes

Julie says: 'When the judges announced a cupcake challenge, I was delighted. Making cupcakes is fun and it takes me back to my childhood and Mum's kitchen. I wanted more than anything to deliver a cake with WOW factor, not only in how it looked but in flavour as well. Lemon is one of my favourite flavours to work with in both savoury and sweet dishes. These cupcakes deliver a lemon hit that will knock your socks off.'

Method

1   Preheat the oven to 180°C (160° fan-forced). Line a 6-hole Texas muffin pan (¾ cup capacity) with paper cases.

2   Using electric beaters, beat the butter, sugar and vanilla extract until light and creamy. Add the eggs, one at a time, beating well between additions. Fold through the flour and milk in two alternate batches until just combined, then gently fold through the lemon zest.

3   Divide the mixture evenly among the paper cases. Bake for about 20 mins, or until cake springs back when touched gently in the centre. Remove from oven and transfer to a wire rack to cool completely before decorating.

4   To make the frosting, use electric beaters to beat the butter until light and creamy. Add the icing sugar a little at a time, beating constantly. Add half the milk and beat until well combined. Add remaining milk if a softer frosting is desired. Spread or pipe onto the cooled cupcakes. Garnish with a small lemon shape cut from a yellow piece of liquorice allsort, or another lemon-flavoured sweet.

Makes 6
Preparation time: 30 mins
Cooking time: 15–20 mins

100 g unsalted butter, softened
¾ cup (165 g) caster sugar
½ tsp vanilla extract
2 eggs
1⅓ cups (200 g) self-raising flour
½ cup (125 ml) milk
zest of 3 lemons

Butter frosting
125 g unsalted butter, softened
1½ cups icing sugar mixture
approx 1 tbs milk

'My signature cupcake's going to be called lemon diva because it's going to look beautiful and be a star, but the flavour will pack a punch.' – Julie, explaining the name of her now-famous lemon diva cupcakes to George

# Kate's Aussie mess

Serves 8
Preparation time: 20 mins
Cooking time: 50 mins

4 eggwhites
1 cup (220 g) caster sugar
4 large ripe mangoes
2 cups (500 ml) thickened cream
4 large bananas
4 passionfruit

Kate says: 'I love making desserts and when I do, I like to play around with the flavours I use. My mother is British and so I have been raised on a lot of delicious British puddings. Eton mess is a classic British pudding consisting of meringue, berries and cream. When I made this dish for Curtis Stone I gave it my own spin using Australian flavours and it was a big hit. The fruits in this dish are seasonal so it's a dessert best saved for a hot summer's day!'

Method

1   Preheat the oven to 120°C (100° fan-forced). Line a baking tray with non-stick baking paper.

2   To make the meringues, beat the eggwhites with electric beaters until soft peaks form. Add the caster sugar gradually, beating until the mixture is stiff and glossy.

3   Spoon large dollops of the mixture onto the prepared tray. They don't have to look pretty because they're going to be broken up into pieces later anyway. Bake for 5 mins and then reduce oven to 100°C (80° fan-forced) and cook for another 45 mins. The initial hotter temperature will help to set the outside of the meringues so that they are crisp on the outside with a chewy centre.

4   Meanwhile, peel the mangoes and cut the flesh from the stone. Puree the flesh in a blender. Transfer to a small saucepan and bring to a simmer. Cook over medium-low heat until it is reduced by half. If the fruit isn't particularly sweet you may like to add a little sugar. Allow to cool.

5   Whip the cream in a large bowl until soft peaks form. Break up the meringues and sprinkle over the cream. Stir to coat the meringue pieces. Divide the mixture between 8 serving glasses. Cut the bananas into 5 mm slices and place over the meringue mixture. Spoon the passionfruit pulp over. To finish, drizzle the mango coulis around the glasses.

# Sticky date pudding with butterscotch sauce and almond praline

Sam, Trevor and Tom performed so well in the sticky date pudding pressure test that the judges didn't have the heart to send any of them home. Matt said he loved the way Tom's praline shattered in the mouth, George said Trevor's butterscotch sauce was liquid gold, and Gary described Sam's pudding as 'fluffy, tasty and jammy'. Three great cooks put up three great puddings and saved their own skins – for a while, at least!

## Method

1   Preheat the oven to 180°C (160° fan-forced). Lightly grease 8 metal dariole moulds (½ cup capacity).

2   Place the dates and 1¼ cups (310 ml) water into a saucepan and bring to the boil over high heat. Remove from the heat. Add the soda and stir until the dates start to break down. Set aside to cool, stirring occasionally to release the heat.

3   Using electric beaters, beat the butter and sugar in a bowl until light and creamy. Add the eggs one at a time, beating well after each addition. Add the date mixture and stir to combine. Carefully fold through the sifted flour. Divide mixture evenly among the prepared moulds.

4   Place the moulds into a baking dish. Carefully pour enough boiling water into the dish to come about ⅓ of the way up the side of the moulds. Bake for 40 mins or until risen, and a skewer comes out clean when inserted into the centre of a pudding.

5   Meanwhile, make the almond praline. Line an oven tray with non-stick baking paper and scatter the almonds over. Combine the sugar and 2 tbs water in a saucepan. Cook over medium heat, swirling the pan but not stirring, until the sugar has dissolved and becomes a deep golden caramel. Pour over the almonds and cool until set, then break into pieces.

6   To make the butterscotch sauce, combine the butter, sugar, cream and vanilla extract in small saucepan. Stir over low heat until the butter melts and the sugar dissolves. Bring to the boil, reduce heat and cook for 5–6 mins, or until the sauce thickens slightly.

7   To serve, invert the hot puddings onto serving plates, then top with butterscotch sauce and shards of praline.

Serves 8
Preparation time: 30 mins
Cooking time: 40 mins

1 cup (170 g) pitted dates, roughly chopped
½ tsp bicarbonate of soda
60 g butter, diced and softened
¾ cup (165 g) firmly packed brown sugar
2 eggs
1 cup (150 g) self-raising flour

Almond praline
¼ cup (35 g) slivered almonds, toasted
½ cup (110 g) caster sugar

Butterscotch sauce
50 g butter
1 cup (220 g) brown sugar
1 cup (250 ml) cream
1 tsp vanilla extract

Recipe by Kirsten Jenkins

# Super-sexy silky-smooth ice-cream

Makes about 1 litre
Preparation time: 10 mins +
 20 mins churning
Cooking time: about 20 mins

2 cups (500 ml) cream
1 vanilla bean, seeds scraped
 and reserved
5 egg yolks
125 g caster sugar

There's nothing better than silky-smooth freshly churned ice-cream – but if you want to make it at home, be prepared to invest in an ice-cream machine. The trick is to use the freshest ingredients possible: fresh eggs, fresh milk, fresh cream. Gary and George taught the contestants a vanilla bean ice-cream recipe and then piped mini-cornets, topping them with pashmak, or Persian fairy floss, as pictured. George suggested that these '007 blonde girls' would have made a super-sexy dessert canapé at the Casino Royale launch night at the Martini Club, when the contestants prepared hors d'oeuvres for a glamorous crowd of partygoers.

Here's a recipe you can use to make ice-cream at home. Once you've mastered plain vanilla, try making chocolate ice-cream by melting 400 g chopped dark chocolate with the cream, or reduce the cream to 1½ cups and add 1 cup sieved berry puree to the cooled custard.

Method

1   Combine the cream, vanilla bean and seeds in a saucepan and slowly bring to the boil.

2   Whisk the egg yolks and sugar together until pale and creamy. Slowly add the cream mixture to the egg yolks, whisking constantly. Pour into a clean saucepan. Stir over low heat for about 20 mins, until the mixture coats the back of a spoon. Don't be tempted to increase the heat to speed up the process, or the custard will curdle.

3   Pour through a fine sieve into a bowl, then stand the bowl over a larger bowl half-filled with ice. Keep whisking to release the heat and cool the custard. Pour the custard into an ice-cream churn, and churn until frozen to a creamy consistency.

# Matt Moran and Andrew Honeysett's warm pear tart

Serves 4
Preparation time: 45 mins
Cooking time: 45 mins

100 g marzipan
1 eggwhite
¼ tsp vanilla extract
½ tsp plain flour
150 g puff pastry
4 Beurre Bosc pears
250 g caster sugar
50 g unsalted butter, melted
2 tsp Pernod
½ tsp fennel seeds
juice of ½ lemon
4 Paradise pears
1 quantity caramel sauce
  (see page 195)
thick cream, to serve
fennel fronds, to garnish

Apple puree
½ vanilla bean
2 large apples, peeled, cored
  and roughly chopped
1 cup (220 g) caster sugar
1 cup (250 ml) dessert wine
  (or water)

Crumble mix
100 g butter
¾ cup (110 g) plain flour
¼ cup (55 g) caster sugar
1 tsp ground ginger

Matt Moran's Sydney restaurant, ARIA, has been awarded two chef's hats an incredible eight times. Matt took on Justine in her second celebrity chef challenge, and the dish he brought to the table – a warm pear tart – came from ARIA's menu. Justine was given a 15-minute head start, but it only took Matt about three minutes to catch up. 'You need to be multi-tasking,' Matt called out to her from his side of the kitchen.

When Justine's tart wasn't cooking properly, Matt took it and put it in his own oven. It puffed up beautifully and Justine took heart – but then everything went to hell. She explained: 'I was concentrating on my pear tart, because I wanted to make that perfect, and I kind of forgot about my crumble.' As Sam observed: 'It was burnt to a cinder – it looked like ground coffee.' With just ten minutes to go, Justine threw together a new crumble mix, then waited as long as she could to plate up so her cream wouldn't melt on the hot crumble. When Matt saw her dish he felt a little nervous: 'Of course I want to win! It's pride and ego on the line here.' But despite Justine's valiant efforts, the judges pronounced plate two, Matt Moran's tart, the winner. His pear had been poached to perfection and the crumble was more intricate in its flavours. Gary nevertheless gave Justine a nine out of ten, telling her that her dish was 'bloody brilliant'.

Method

1   Combine the Pernod, fennel seeds, lemon juice and 220 g sugar in a saucepan with 1⅔ cup (415 ml) water and bring to the boil. Peel and core the Paradise pears and add to the pan. Cover with foil or baking paper to keep them submerged. Simmer for about 10 mins, until tender.

2   To make the apple puree, scrape the seeds from the vanilla bean and place the bean and seeds into a saucepan with the remaining ingredients. Cover and bring to a simmer. Cook for 10–15 mins, until soft. Drain the excess liquid, remove the vanilla bean and puree the mixture with a stick blender. Pass the puree through a fine sieve. Refrigerate until cold. Spoon into a squeeze bottle.

3   Preheat the oven to 200°C (180° fan-forced) and line a baking tray with non-stick baking paper. Beat the marzipan, eggwhite, vanilla extract and flour in a bowl until smooth. Roll the puff pastry out onto a floured work surface into a 16 cm x 22 cm rectangle. The pastry should be no thicker than 5 mm. Place the pastry on the prepared tray and spread with a thin layer of the marzipan mixture.

4   Peel the Beurre Bosc pears and cut in half lengthways. Using a teaspoon or melon baller, remove the cores. Cut into slices about 2–3 mm thick. Lay the pear slices, overlapping each other, onto the puff pastry to cover. Sprinkle over 30 g of the caster sugar and drizzle with the melted butter. Bake for 15 mins.

5   To make the crumble mix, place all the ingredients in a bowl and rub in the butter until it resembles breadcrumbs. Place the crumb mixture on a baking tray and bake for about 8 mins – tossing halfway through to ensure even cooking – until golden brown.

6   Remove the tart from the oven. Spoon half of the caramel sauce evenly over the tart. Place a sheet of baking paper on top of the tart and then place a baking tray on top. Flip the tart over so the sliced pear is on the bottom of the tray. Return to the oven and cook for a further 10–15 mins. Remove the tart from the oven and flip over again. Transfer the tart from the baking sheet to a chopping board. The pears should be golden brown and caramelised.

7   To serve, squeeze a line of the apple puree along a serving plate in a zigzag. Cut the tart into 3 cm x 7 cm slices. Place a slice on the line of puree. Spoon 1 tsp of the cold caramel sauce onto the plate and drag it slightly. Next place one spoon of the crumble mix on plate, quenelle a spoonful of cream and sit it on top of the crumble. Drain the Paradise pear and, using a paring knife, cut it into 2 or 3 pieces. Cut a tiny slit in one piece and poke in a frond of fennel, then place it on the plate to serve.

# Adriano Zumbo's croquembouche

Serves about 30
Preparation time: 2 hours
Cooking time: about 40 mins

1 quantity choux pastry batter
  (see page 197)
1 quantity pastry cream
  (see page 194)
hail sugar
violets, to decorate

Caramel
660 g caster sugar
260 ml liquid glucose

SAFETY TIP
Always have a bowl of cold water on the bench when you are making toffee or caramel. Submerge any burn in the water immediately.

'When Adriano carried his croquembouche out I thought all my internal organs were going to shut down. I was terrified, absolutely terrified. I'd never made anything like that in my life.' – Julie

Poh, Chris, Tom and Julie were given just two hours and fifteen minutes to reproduce Adriano Zumbo's magnificent mountain of profiteroles filled with crème pâtissière, bound with caramel, wrapped in spun sugar and studded with tiny violets. Poh says: 'It was the most ridiculous task. It shaved two years off my life at least.'

Method

1   To make the choux puffs, preheat the oven to 210°C (190° fan-forced). Lightly grease 4 large baking trays. Spoon half of the choux pastry batter into a piping bag fitted with a 1.25–1.5 cm nozzle. Cover the remaining pastry with cling film. Pipe the mixture onto the trays in mounds 3 cm wide and 2 cm high, leaving 5 cm between them for spreading. Bake, in batches, for 25–30 mins, until puffed and golden brown. They should feel firm and sound hollow when tapped. Transfer the puffs to wire racks to cool, and repeat with remaining pastry.

2   Spoon the pastry cream into a piping bag with a nozzle less than 1 cm. Poke a small hole in the base of each puff and fill with the cream.

3   To make the caramel, stir the sugar in a saucepan with 200 ml water, without boiling, until sugar dissolves. Bring to the boil without stirring. Add the glucose. Cook until the mixture is caramel in colour. Remove from the heat and dip the base of the pan in a bowl of cold water to cool slightly. Grease a cake ring (slightly larger than the base of the croquembouche cone), and place on a tray lined with baking paper. Pour in enough caramel to coat the base to a depth of 5 mm. This is the base for the croquembouche.

4   Dip the base of each puff in toffee, and then dip some in hail sugar. Place them upside down on trays lined with baking paper to set.

5   To assemble, oil the inside of a croquembouche cone. (You can hire these from kitchenware shops.) Place one uncoated puff into the point of the cone. Working one at a time, dip the sides of the puff balls into the toffee and place into the cone. Continue dipping and adding balls until the inside of the cone is covered. Leave to set.

6   Transfer the base for the croquembouche to a serving plate. Place a small amount of caramel on the puffs around the base of the cone. Invert the cone onto the base and lift it off gently. Reheat the remaining caramel, then dip two forks in it, back to back. Spin toffee around the croquembouche. Decorate with violets.

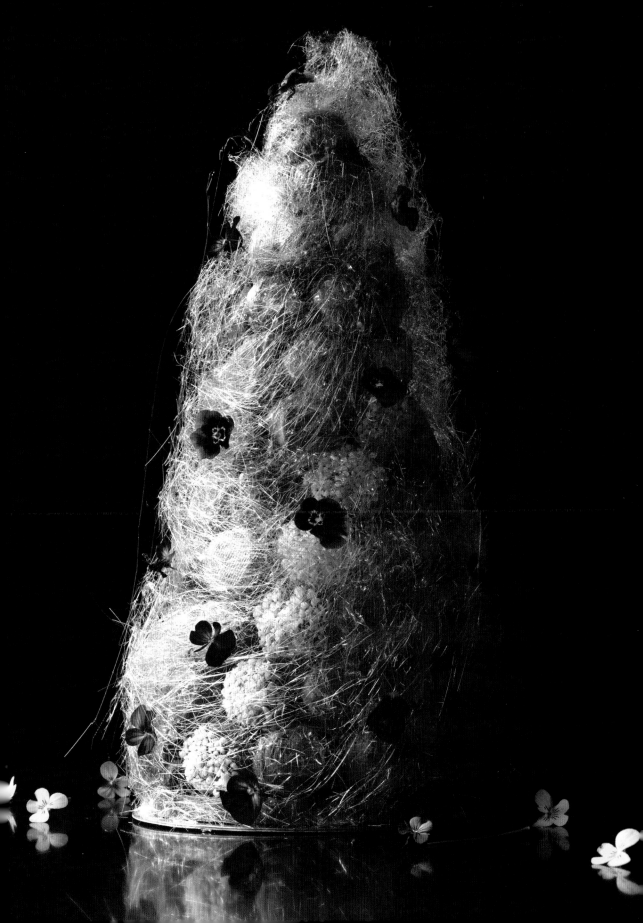

# Linda's blueberry and violet rice pudding

Linda says: 'This dessert was my dish for the very first day of auditions, and I chose it because it represents my family, our culture and traditions. Blueberry picking is our annual family outing in the summer and I couldn't help but use such amazing seasonal produce.

'What makes this dessert truly special to me is its humour – my brother Chris nicknamed me "Blueberry" because I have always been a constant nibbler and I reminded him of Violet from the movie *Willy Wonka*. She eventually inflated into a big blueberry!'

Method

1. To make the rice pudding, whisk the vanilla seeds, rice and milk in a small saucepan and bring to the boil. Reduce the heat to low and gently simmer, whisking often, for 20 mins. Whisking allows the rice starch to thicken the milk and make the pudding creamier. The rice should still be al dente. In a separate bowl, whisk the sugar and yolks together. Slowly pour one-third of the rice pudding into the egg mixture, whisking constantly. Return the mixture to the saucepan, along with the blueberries. Simmer on the lowest possible heat for 5 mins. Set aside, cover and rest for 10 mins. This will allow the rice to soften but not overcook.

2. To make the violet shortbread dots, preheat the oven to 170°C (150° fan-forced). Line a small tray with non-stick baking paper. Using an apple corer or 2–3 cm round cutter, cut out as many dots as possible from the pastry. Using a paring knife, cut small fragments of the candied violets and press them into the dots. Bake the dot biscuits for 5 mins or until lightly coloured. Remove from the oven and allow to cool.

3. To make the violet syrup, combine the sugar, cordial and 1 tbs water in a small saucepan. Stir to dissolve the sugar, then simmer for 5 mins or until the syrup coats the back of a spoon. Set aside.

4. To make the blueberry sauce, combine the blueberries and sugar with 2 tbs water in a small saucepan. Stir to dissolve the sugar, then poach over a low heat for 5 mins.

5. To serve, mix ¼ cup of the violet syrup through the pudding and spoon into glasses, then pour over a little of the blueberry sauce. Top with shaved white chocolate and place glasses on serving plates. Make little dots of violet syrup on the plate and place a blueberry on top of each one. Pipe dots of mascarpone onto the plate and top with fresh violets, then arrange the violet shortbread dots among them.

Serves 4
Preparation time: 1 hour
Cooking time: 30 mins

Rice pudding
1 vanilla pod, split lengthways and seeds scraped
½ cup (110 g) vialone nano or arborio rice
2 cups (500 ml) full-cream milk
2 tbs sugar
2 egg yolks
½ cup (70 g) fresh or frozen blueberries (or 3 tbs blueberry jam)

Violet shortbread dots
½ sheet frozen sweet shortcrust pastry, thawed
4 candied violets

Violet syrup
2 tbs sugar
5 tbs violet cordial (also known as Monin Violette)

Blueberry sauce
½ cup blueberries
1 tbs sugar

To decorate
white chocolate, curled at room temperature using a sharp knife
mascarpone
fresh violets
fresh blueberries

# Tarte tatin

The French classic, tarte tatin, is an apple tart baked upside down, with the apples on the bottom and the pastry on top. It seems as if it should be easy to cook, but it's not. Gary told Aaron, Linda and Julie, the bottom three in the Italian invention test, that the judges had chosen tarte tatin for the pressure test because it was a high-risk dish that could go wrong right up to the last minute, and would really show what they were capable of. If you're methodical and stick carefully to the recipe, you should be fine, but be careful not to cut your apples too thin. Linda was the sorry one sent home that day, and that was the mistake she made.

## Method

1  Preheat the oven to 220°C (200° fan-forced). Peel the apples and cut into quarters. Remove the cores (cutting each quarter at the core so it has a 'flat' side), and toss in a large bowl with the lemon juice and 1 tbs of the sugar.

2  Using a 20 cm frying pan as a guide, cut the pastry into a round slightly larger than the pan. Prick all over with a fork.

3  Melt the butter in a 20 cm non-stick frying pan (with an ovenproof handle) over medium-high heat. Sprinkle with the remaining sugar. Reduce the heat to medium-low, and cook until a rich caramel forms. Shake the pan occasionally to spread around any dark spots that appear.

4  Arrange the apple quarters in a circular pattern in the pan, rounded side down. Cut any remaining quarters into pieces to fill the gaps. Cook the apples over medium heat for about 10 mins, until caramel is bubbling up in the pan. Shake the pan occasionally to prevent burnt spots.

5  Carefully lay the pastry over the apples and tuck in the overhanging edge. Place the pan into the oven and cook for about 25 mins, or until the puff pastry has risen and cooked. The pastry should be golden brown and flaky. Stand the tarte in the pan for 10 mins before carefully turning out onto a serving plate. Serve with cream.

Serves 2
Preparation time: 15 mins
Cooking time: 40 mins +
  10 mins standing

3 Golden Delicious apples
1 tbs lemon juice
½ cup (110 g) caster sugar
1 sheet ready-rolled puff pastry
20 g unsalted butter, chopped
cream, to serve

Recipe by Kate Nichols

'Follow the recipe to the tee. Don't vary it, don't move it, don't do anything other than what the hell's on that recipe.'
– Aaron

## MasterTip

'When it's rested for ten minutes, you should be able to put your hand on the top of the tarte and spin it round. This is a really important part of the whole process. If it doesn't move, it's stuck.' – Gary

221

# Adriano Zumbo's vanilla pannacotta with macarons

When Adriano Zumbo appeared on the MasterChef set for the second time, the contestants were wary. They knew him as the evil genius behind the infamous croquembouche pressure test. This time he came bearing a caramelised tonka bean pannacotta sitting atop a passionfruit slick and garnished with two macarons, one filled with jasmine rice pudding ganache and the other with a pine nut ganache. André, Poh, Sam and Chris had 90 minutes to recreate the dish.

Everyone but Poh had trouble with the macarons. André's were flat and he complained that plating them up was like standing a frisbee on its end. The quantities in this recipe are enough to give you spares, in case some of them don't pop or 'kick' the way they should. Unmoulding the pannacotta was the other problem the contestants faced; you need to give the mould a good squeeze to introduce some air. Don't try this dessert for the first time when you're holding a dinner party for people you want to impress – give it a couple of trial runs to be sure you know what you're doing!

Serves 4
Preparation time: 30 mins
Cooking time: 1½ hours

## Pannacotta
120 g caster sugar
1 vanilla bean, split, seeds
  scraped
¼ grated tonka bean
500 ml cream
2 gelatine leaves (4 g)

## Macaron
150 g caster sugar
55 g eggwhites, plus 55 g
  eggwhites, extra (see note)
1 g powdered eggwhite
150 g almond meal
150 g pure icing sugar
light brown food colouring
ground cinnamon, for dusting
pine nuts, to decorate

## Jasmine rice pudding ganache
60 g jasmine rice
250 ml cream
90 ml milk
45 g caster sugar
65 g brown sugar
1 vanilla bean, split, seeds
  scraped
1 tsp finely grated orange zest
50 ml cream, extra
85 g white chocolate, chopped
pinch ground cinnamon
25 g butter

## Pine nut and chocolate ganache
60 ml cream
100 g white chocolate, chopped
20 g dark chocolate, chopped
25 g pine nut paste, plus a
  little extra for garnish
35 g butter
½ tsp sea salt

## Passionfruit oil slick
2 tsp lemon juice
75 ml strained passionfruit pulp
100 g caster sugar
2 eggs
150 ml extra-virgin
  olive oil

## To decorate
fresh raspberries
dried rose petals
toasted pine nuts
pine nut paste
pistachio paste
gold leaf

# Adriano Zumbo's vanilla pannacotta with macarons

'A great pannacotta totters and wobbles like a Rubenesque woman on five-inch stilettos . . . Gorgeous!' – Matt

'I don't know what to say. There's no way I can cook that!' – Sam

'Oh my god, Adriano Zumbo is like the bringer of all my pain!' – Poh

Method

1   To make the pannacotta, combine the sugar and the vanilla seeds and tonka bean in a saucepan. Cook over medium heat until the sugar has melted and the mixture is caramel in colour. Meanwhile, heat the cream in a small saucepan, then add the warm cream to the caramel. Stir to combine. Remove from heat. Soak the gelatine leaf in cold water until soft, then squeeze out the excess moisture. Stir the gelatine into the cream mixture and strain through a sieve placed over a small bowl. Cool to room temperature. Pour into four ½ cup (125 ml) plastic dariole moulds. Refrigerate for 1 hour or until set.

2   To make the macarons, preheat the oven to 200°C (180° fan-forced) and line 2 baking trays with non-stick baking paper. Place another tray underneath each tray, to give a double thickness. Make an Italian meringue by combining 40 ml water with the caster sugar in a saucepan and cook till 121°C on a sugar thermometer. Beat 55 g eggwhites and the powdered eggwhite in a bowl with electric beaters until soft peaks form. Slowly add the hot sugar syrup to the eggwhite while beating continuously (pour the sugar syrup to the side of the bowl slowly).

3   Sift the almond meal and icing sugar together and add the extra 55 g eggwhites. Add to the meringue. In a folding motion, slap the mixture to knock out the air. Divide the mixture into two bowls. Add a drop of light brown colour to one bowl. Spoon mixtures into piping bags each fitted with a 1 cm round nozzle. Pipe 4 cm rounds of each coloured macaron onto the prepared trays. Tap the tray gently on the bench to remove any excess air from the mixture. Dust the white macarons with cinnamon, and top the light-brown macarons with a pine nut. Leave macarons to air-dry till they form a skin on the surface. Place into the oven and turn off the heat for 6 mins. Turn the oven on to 160°C (140° fan-forced) and cook for about 10 mins, or until a macaron can be lifted from the tray (it should be still soft to touch underneath).

4   To make the jasmine rice pudding ganache, combine the rice, cream, milk, sugars, vanilla seeds (reserve a small pinch) and bean and orange rind in a saucepan. Cook over low heat for about 30 mins, until the rice is cooked but still a little al dente. Heat the extra cream in a small saucepan. Place the chocolate, cinnamon and reserved vanilla seeds into a bowl and pour in the hot cream. Stir until smooth. Stir in the butter. Add chocolate mixture to the rice pudding. Fold to combine.

5   To make the pine nut and chocolate ganache, heat the cream in a small saucepan. Place the chocolate in a bowl with the pine nut paste and pour over the hot cream. Stir in the butter and salt until smooth.

6   To make the passionfruit oil slick, combine the lemon juice, passionfruit pulp, sugar and eggs in a bowl. Cook until sugar thermometer reaches 85°C. Strain through a sieve placed over a bowl, then cool to 45°C, stirring continuously. Drizzle in olive oil in a slow stream, whisking constantly (like making a mayonnaise).

7   To fill the macarons, place each ganache into a piping bag. Sandwich light-brown macarons with pine nut ganache, and cinnamon-dusted macarons with rice pudding ganache. (Take care, as they are very fragile.)

8   To assemble the dish, spoon a little of the passionfruit oil slick onto a serving plate. Top with 1 tsp pistachio paste and rake with a plastic comb across the plate. Invert the pannacotta onto the plate. Add 2 macarons (one of each colour), and decorate with fresh raspberries, rose petals, toasted pine nuts, pine nut paste and gold leaf.

Note Tonka beans are from South America. They should be used sparingly and only as directed in the recipe, as too much can cause health problems. They are available from spice specialists (look online). Omit from the recipe if desired.

Note A standard 59 g egg yields about 35 g of eggwhite. The best idea is to lightly whisk the eggwhites (this makes it easier to take some out if necessary), then weigh them to get the exact amount.

'A macaron should be generous, like a big four-wheel-drive tyre.' – Matt

'I remember being an apprentice and making pistachio macarons for the first time. I think they all ended up in the bin.' – Gary

'The macarons look like an innocent little biscuit, but there's a hell of a lot going on in there.' – Chris

'The macaron mixture was runny, it was gooey, it was all over my fingers, it was sticky, it was running straight out the bottom of the piping bag, out the hole. It just had no shape. I was in a bit of trouble at that stage.' – André

'Let's face it, this is an extremely complicated dish. Let's not joke around here. Don't underestimate it.' – George

# Julie's brutti ma buono

Julie says: 'These lovely chewy, nutty meringues are made in a different way to other meringue dishes I have attempted. They are first par-cooked in a pot. It looks like an unlikely sticky mess, even after they are baked, hence the name, which means 'ugly but good'. I enjoyed the fact that the title of this dish took pressure off me to present something perfect and symmetrical and refined – these biscuits really are ugly. But they also really are good.'

## Method

1   Preheat the oven to 180°C (160° fan-forced). Line an oven tray with baking paper. Place whole walnuts on tray. Dust with ¼ cup (40 g) of the icing sugar and sprinkle with half of the Grand Marnier. Bake for 15 mins or until golden, then remove candied walnuts from oven. Reduce temperature to 150°C (130° fan-forced).

2   Beat eggwhites and caster sugar with electric beaters until stiff peaks form. Fold through chopped toasted walnuts and vanilla essence. Cook in saucepan over low heat until light golden brown. Spoon 16 mounds of mixture onto baking trays lined with baking paper. Bake for 30 mins. Cool.

3   Beat cream and remaining icing sugar with electric beaters until soft peaks form. Fold through raspberries and remaining Grand Marnier.

4   Sandwich walnut meringues together with raspberry cream. Serve with candied walnuts, extra cream and whole raspberries.

Serves 8
Preparation time: 20 mins
Cooking time: 30 mins

½ cup (60 g) whole walnuts
⅓ cup (55 g) icing sugar
2 tbs Grand Marnier
4 eggwhites
1 tbs caster sugar
1½ cups (180 g) finely chopped toasted walnuts
½ tsp vanilla essence
300 ml pure cream
125 g punnet raspberries, chopped
extra cream and whole raspberries, to serve

# Aaron's raspberry, lychee and rose ispahan

Aaron says: 'This recipe is very close to my heart, as it is the reason for me being where I am today. I made the ispahan for my very first MasterChef audition. The word ispahan is normally used to describe a Persian-style rug with ornamental and floral patterns on a deep coloured background, but in this instance it is used to describe the deep colours and floral nature of this dessert. I have developed the idea and turned the creation into a full restaurant-style dessert, influenced by Terry Clarke, my head chef at Persimmon restaurant, who constantly reminds me that food and fine dining is all about finesse.'

Serves 2
Preparation time: 3 days
Cooking time: 1 hour

## Ispahan macaron
110 g almond meal
200 g pure icing sugar
96 g eggwhites (leave in a covered bowl at room temperature overnight, then refrigerate for 2 days for best results)
drop lemon juice
pinch salt
30 g caster sugar
2 tsp freeze-dried raspberry powder (FD140)

## Ispahan buttercream
⅓ cup (75 g) caster sugar
60g eggwhites (see note)
120 g unsalted butter, diced, at room temperature
½ tsp lychee juice (see note)
1 tsp rosewater

## Goats' milk ice-cream
1 cup (250 ml) goats' milk
1 cup (250 g) double cream
4 egg yolks
¼ cup (55 g) caster sugar
1 tsp vanilla bean paste

## Rose and lychee fluid gel
185 ml lychee juice (see note)
1 tbs rosewater
2.5 g agar agar

## Raspberry soil
50 g raspberry powder FD140
94 g plain flour
87 g caster sugar
2 g fine salt
94 g unsalted butter, chopped, at room temperature

## Crystallised rose petals
8 rose petals, washed and dried (or pesticide-free from a florist)
150 g eggwhites (see note), lightly beaten
50 g icing sugar

## To serve
16 raspberries
8 fresh or canned lychees, cut into quarters
1 tbs toasted coriander seed, finely ground

Method

1   To make the macarons, preheat the oven to 145°C (125°C fan-forced). Line a baking tray with non-stick baking paper. Preheat the tray in the oven for around 5–10 mins. Sift the almond meal and icing sugar into a large mixing bowl.

2   Place the eggwhites in a large bowl with the lemon juice and salt. Whisk to soft peaks, then gradually add the caster sugar, whisking until dissolved between each addition. Sift in the raspberry powder. The mixture should be thick and glossy.

3   Using a spatula, fold half of the almond mixture into the meringue. When it is combined, fold in the remaining almond mixture. Do not over-mix – the process should take no more than 40 strokes in total. Transfer the mixture to a piping bag and pipe six 5 cm diameter rounds onto the warm tray. You will only need 4, but this will give you 2 spares. Rest this mixture on the baking sheet for 1 hour so that a skin forms, ensuring your macarons have 'feet'. Bake for 12–14 mins. Cool completely on the tray, then carefully remove and store in a cool dry place. Be careful, as they will be very delicate.

4   To make the buttercream, place the sugar and the eggwhites in a heat-proof bowl, then stir gently until combined. Place the bowl over small pan of simmering water and stir gently until the sugar has dissolved and the mixture is warm. Remove the bowl from the heat and whisk until soft peaks form. Whisking constantly, add the butter a little at a time. Whisk in the lychee juice and rosewater. Refrigerate for 40 mins. Remove from the fridge and return to room temperature (not too warm) before using.

# Aaron's raspberry, lychee & rose ispahan

5   To make the goats' milk ice-cream, combine the milk and cream in a small saucepan. Bring just to the boil and remove from the heat. In a metal mixing bowl, whisk the egg yolks with the sugar and vanilla paste until creamy. Very gradually whisk in ½ cup (125 ml) of the hot milk mixture. Once well incorporated, whisk in remainder of the milk mixture. Pour into a clean saucepan and stir over medium heat for about 4 mins, until the mixture thickens. Sieve the mixture through a fine chinois into a stainless steel bowl, placed over a bowl filled with ice. Whisk until well chilled. Churn in an ice-cream machine, or place the bowl over the bowl of ice together in the freezer, and whisk every 5–10 mins until frozen.

6   To make the rose and lychee fluid gel, place all the ingredients in a medium saucepan and mix with a stick blender. Bring to the boil, then reduce the heat to medium. Simmer for 5 mins. Take off the heat, pour into a small bowl and refrigerate until set. Put the set gel into a blender and blend until smooth and fluid. Refrigerate until ready to use.

7   To make the raspberry soil, preheat the oven to 135°C and line a baking tray with non-stick baking paper. Combine the raspberry powder, flour, sugar and salt in a mixing bowl. Add the butter and, using electric beaters or a wooden spoon, mix until large crumbs form. Spread the mixture out onto the prepared baking tray. Bake, rotating the pan halfway through cooking, for about 20 mins, until crisp. Set aside to cool completely, then blitz in a food processor for 5 seconds to make fine soil. Store in an airtight container.

8   To make the crystallised rose petals, line a tray with non-stick baking paper. Use a pair of tweezers to dip the petals gently into the eggwhites, evenly coating. Drain off the excess. Sift the icing sugar over the petal on both sides to coat, and shake gently to remove any excess. Place onto the prepared tray to dry. It is advisable to do these a day or at least a couple of hours in advance.

9   To assemble the ispahan, spread the buttercream onto a macaron. Gently place raspberries on the buttercream, around the outside edge, and arrange half the lychee quarters in the centre. Pipe some more buttercream on top of the lychee, and sandwich a second macaron on top.

10  To serve, pipe a large dot of the fluid gel onto serving plates, and top with the ispahan. Arrange a raspberry and rose petal on top. Make a couple of delicate lines of toasted coriander powder. Pipe small dots of the fluid gel onto the plate, smearing every second one, and placing a rose petal on the others. Spread a thick line of raspberry soil onto the plate, and top with a quenelle of the ice-cream. Sprinkle with a little more raspberry soil, and serve.

Note To make the lychee juice, blend ½ cup of tinned lychees with ½ of cup of the syrup they are preserved in.

Note A standard 59 g egg yields about 35 g of eggwhite. The best idea is to lightly whisk the eggwhites (this makes it easier to take some out if necessary), then weigh them to get the exact amount.

# Geni's baklava

Serves 20
Preparation time: 1 hour
Cooking time: 1 hour 10 mins

375 g packet filo pastry
250 g butter
whole cloves, to stud each
  triangle of baklava

Baklava filling
1½ cups (180 g) finely
  chopped walnuts
1½ cup (180 g) finely
  chopped almonds
¼ cup (14 g) fresh breadcrumbs
1 tbs sugar
2 tsp ground cinnamon
1 tsp ground cloves

Syrup
1 cup (250 ml) honey
1 cup (220 g) caster sugar
1 cinnamon stick
finely grated zest of one lemon
squeeze of lemon juice
4–6 whole cloves

Geni says: 'Baklava is a *glyko*, or sweet, eaten on very special occasions such as name day celebrations, christenings, weddings and holidays. It is a filo pastry filled with nuts and drenched in syrup. Women in Greece frequently prepare and assemble their baklava at home and then carry their *tapsi* (round baking dish) to the local baker to be baked crisp to perfection.

'Syrup flavourings vary. Honey with lemon peel, lemon juice, cinnamon and cloves are common ingredients in Greece. Cool syrup is generally poured over baklava hot from the oven, but I prefer to add hot syrup to cool baklava for maximum flakiness.'

Method

1  Preheat the oven to 160°C (140° fan-forced). To make the filling, combine all the ingredients in a large bowl.

2  Oil the base and sides of a 50 cm x 30 cm (or similar) rectangular baking pan. Brush a sheet of filo with a little melted butter and place into the pan, allowing any extra to hang over the sides. Repeat to make 8 layers of pastry.

3  Spoon one-third of the nut mixture evenly over the pastry. Brush 2 more sheets of pastry with butter and layer into the pan. Repeat layering with remaining filling and double sheets of buttered pastry, finishing with a triple layer of pastry. Tuck in the overhanging pastry. Reserve remaining pastry sheets for another use.

4  Using a sharp knife, score the filo pastry into triangle shapes (score it first into squares, and then in half diagonally to make triangles). Cut again along the scored lines, this time cutting all the way through. Press a whole clove into the middle of each triangle. Bake for about 1 hour 10 mins or until golden.

5  To make the syrup, combine all the ingredients with 1 cup (250 ml) water in a medium saucepan and stir over medium heat, without boiling, until the sugar has dissolved. Bring to the boil, then reduce the heat and simmer for 15 mins. Strain, then pour over the cooled baklava.

Note
Baklava can be prepared and baked the day before. The hot syrup can be added on the day of serving.

# Adriano Zumbo's chocolate mousse cake

Adriano Zumbo's chocolate mousse cake was the only thing standing between Chris, Poh, Justine, Julie and a place in the top three. By now the contestants knew that a Zumbo dessert was bound to be a challenge. Poh had been given a sneak peek at the recipe, but didn't feel that was a significant advantage. 'I think you guys should be quite scared right now,' she told the others. 'We are about to enter a world of pain.' And she wasn't just trying to psyche them out.

The layers in this cake are best made the day before assembly. Once you've assembled them, put the cake in the freezer overnight. Adriano says this cake is all about the ooze, so don't be too concerned when your caramel starts flowing as it begins to thaw.

Serves 8
Preparation time: 1½ hours +
  2 nights freezing
Cooking time: 2½ hours

### Cinnamon pâté sable
285 g cold butter, diced
185 g caster sugar
375 g plain flour
2 g ground cinnamon
¼ vanilla bean, seeds scraped
1 egg, lightly beaten

### Apple filling
400 g caster sugar
185 g butter
7 Granny Smith apples,
  peeled and diced
zest of 1 orange, finely grated
6 g fresh ginger, chopped
15 ml calvados

### Salted caramel
220 g cream
300 g caster sugar
60 g glucose
5 g gelatine leaves
25 g unsalted butter
2 g sea salt flakes

### Biscuit decor jaconde
cigarette decor paste (see below)
3 eggs
100 g icing sugar
100 g almond meal
90 g eggwhites (see note)
45 g caster sugar
20 g butter, melted
30 g plain flour

### Cigarette decor paste
50 ml cream
50 g eggwhites (see note)
50 g icing sugar
30 g plain flour
20 g cocoa

### Chocolate blackberry ganache
60 g blackberry puree
25 g caster sugar
6 g inverted sugar
3 g caster sugar, extra
1.5 g pectin nh
100 g 64% dark chocolate,
  broken into small pieces
17 g butter

### Sabayon mousse
60 ml strained black tea
50 g caster sugar
50 g egg
blackberry ganache (see above)
60 g 64% dark chocolate
400 ml cream, whipped to
  soft peaks

### Tempered chocolate curl
500 g white chocolate
80 g cocoa butter
yellow liposoluble food colour

### Chocolate spray
500 g dark chocolate
350 g cocoa butter

### To decorate
whole hazelnuts
edible silver metallic dust

'If you thought the
croquembouche test was tough,
this is another whole level.
Adriano, on a scale of one to
ten, how hard is this dish?'
– Matt

'Ten.' – Adriano

'*Who* makes desserts like that??'
– Poh

'We've got nine different
opportunities here to screw up.
There's so much going on it's
hard to get your head around it.'
– Chris

'Don't forget the jaconde, yeah!'
– Gary

Method

1   To make the cinnamon pâté sable, preheat oven to 180°C (160°C
    fan-forced). Place the butter, sugar, flour, cinnamon and vanilla in a
    food processor and process until the mixture resembles fine crumbs.
    Add the egg and process until the mixture comes together in small
    lumps. Tip the mixture onto a lightly floured workbench and knead
    lightly. Roll out on a sheet of non-stick baking paper until 7–8 mm
    thick. Place a 20 cm ring mould over the pastry and cut around the
    outside edge. Remove the excess outer pastry. Transfer the pastry and
    ring mould onto an oven tray lined with baking paper and bake for
    about 20 mins, until lightly golden.

2   To make the apple filling, spread 350 g of the sugar over the base of
    a non-stick frying pan and cook over medium-low heat until melted
    and caramelised. Add half the butter and stir to combine. Add 4 of
    the apples and cook until they are translucent and caramel in colour.
    Cool the mixture and set aside. Next combine the orange zest, ginger
    and remaining butter in a large frying pan and cook until aromatic.
    Add the remaining sugar and apples. Cook over high heat for 1
    min, add calvados and flambé. Cool, and then combine the 2 apple
    mixtures together. Place into an 18 cm silicone mould and freeze
    overnight until set.

3   To make the salted caramel layer, heat the cream until hot, then
    set aside. Place sugar, glucose and 120 ml water in a saucepan and
    cook over medium-low heat until the sugar has dissolved and the
    mixture is a caramel colour. Deglaze with the cream and stir until
    smooth. Soak the gelatine leaves in cold water until soft, squeeze
    out the excess moisture, then add them to the caramel mixture.
    Cool to 50°C. Add the butter and salt and blitz with a stick blender
    until smooth and shiny. Place in an 18 cm silicone mould and freeze
    overnight until set.

4   To make the biscuit decor jaconde, preheat the oven to 180°C
    (160° fan-forced) and line two oven trays with non-stick baking
    paper. First make the cigarette decor paste. Mix all the ingredients
    together and place on the prepared trays, then swirl a pattern in the
    mixture with your fingers and place it in the freezer. Next make the
    jaconde. Whisk the eggs, icing sugar and almond meal together.
    Beat the eggwhites until soft peaks form, then add the caster sugar
    gradually, beating to stiff peaks. Fold the eggwhites into the almond
    mixture, alternating with butter and flour. Using a pastry scraper or
    palette knife, spread the cigarette paste with a thin layer (about 3mm
    thick) of jaconde. These need to be large enough to cut an 18 cm
    circle from each, and a 15 cm long, 5 cm wide piece as well. Bake for
    10–15 mins, until lightly golden. Cool.

5   To make the chocolate blackberry sabayon mousse, first make the chocolate blackberry ganache. Heat the blackberry puree in a saucepan. Add the sugar and inverted sugar, stir to dissolve and bring to the boil. Add the extra sugar and the pectin. Pour the mixture over the chocolate in a heat-proof bowl and stir until melted and smooth. Cool to 40°C, add the butter and blend with a stick blender.

6   To make the sabayon mousse, place the tea, sugar and eggs into a heat-proof bowl over a pan of simmering water. Using electric beaters, beat until the mixture is light, creamy and mousse-like. Melt the chocolate and stir into the blackberry ganache. Whisk in the cream, then gently fold through the sabayon.

7   To make the tempered chocolate curl, first melt half the chocolate in a heat-proof bowl over a saucepan of simmering water. Keep adding more chocolate, stirring, until it reaches 30°C. To test if the chocolate has tempered correctly, dip a small square of non-stick baking paper in it. Place the paper on a workbench in a cool place. The chocolate on it should set with a smooth, glossy appearance and a crisp snap.

8   Next, temper the cocoa butter by melting it in a saucepan and then pouring it onto a clean work surface to cool rapidly (around 32°C). Add the food colour as soon as you pour the cocoa butter on the table and work it in with the palette knife. When cool, brush onto clear plastic, working left to right, and keep brushing in the same direction as it thickens to obtain brush strokes. Cover in tempered white chocolate and then cut it into strips. Curl or bend to desired shape, as pictured, then leave to set.

9   To assemble the cake, arrange the strip of jaconde around the inside wall of a 20 cm cake ring. Spread the mousse across the base, then up the sides, smoothing so there are no air pockets. Next make a layer of the caramel. Cut an 18 cm disc of jaconde and place it over the caramel, then spread another layer of mousse. Next make a layer of the apple, then another disc of jaconde, and a final layer of mousse. Finish with the sable. Place in the freezer overnight to set.

10  To make the chocolate spray, melt the cocoa butter and add the chocolate. Stir until melted and smooth, then cool to 40°C. (Make the spray close to time of use.) Transfer to a spray gun.

11  To serve, invert the cake onto a serving plate. (Use a warm cloth over the mould to help loosen it.) Spray with the chocolate spray and place the white chocolate curl on top. Cover a few hazelnuts with metallic dust and use them to decorate the cake.

Note A standard 59 g egg yields about 35 g of eggwhite. The best idea is to lightly whisk the eggwhites (this makes it easier to take some out if necessary), then weigh them to get the exact amount.

'First there's a layer of mousse. The next layer is the caramel disc, then there's a layer of jaconde, which is very fragile, then there's a layer of mousse, a layer of apple, then there's a layer of jaconde, then there's another layer of mousse, and then the sable.' – Julie

'You have to make sure everything fits nice and snug or else it just won't hold together.' – Justine

'The blast freezer is your friend. Use it.' – Adriano

'I turned my cake over and it was a total disaster. All the dimples were just horrible craters of mess and my head just caved in and I kind of gave up at the end. It was chaos. The sound of the spray guns is quite loud, and you do feel a little bit like you're in a hardware shop.' – Poh

'Tell you what, to go through *that* experience of making *that* cake . . . I'm never gonna forget that, ever.' – Justine

# Chris's beeramisu

Chris says: 'Beeramisu is an old favourite for cooking-with-beer enthusiasts. The success of the dish largely depends on the quality of the beer and the mascarpone. You need to let the flavours develop over at least two to three hours, though I challenge you to keep your spoons out of it for any longer than that. I love introducing people to this dish as they are always stunned to discover that beer can be used in this manner. Although I know how great this tastes, it was nerve-wracking showing the judges a beery twist on an old, Italian classic.'

Serves 8–10
Preparation time: 20 mins
Chilling time: 2–3 hours

6 eggs, separated
¼ cup (55 g) caster sugar
500 g mascarpone (get the best you can afford – it makes a difference)
1 cup (250 ml) stout, preferably coffee or chocolate stout
½ cup (125 ml) brewed coffee
24 sponge fingers, or alternatively use Italian-style amaretti biscuits
Dutch cocoa, for dusting

'Brilliant. I could eat the whole glass.' – Gary

'Beeramisu! It could be a Chris classic to replace an Italian classic . . .' – Matt

Method

1   Using electric beaters, beat the eggs yolks with the caster sugar until they are pale and thick, then mix in the mascarpone.

2   Using clean beaters, beat the eggwhites until soft peaks form. Carefully fold into the mascarpone mixture.

3   Mix the stout and coffee together and dunk the biscuits, one at a time, into the liquid. (If using the softer sponge fingers make it a quick dunk, as you don't want the biscuits to go soggy.) Layer the biscuits into serving glasses, followed by a thick layer of mascarpone mixture. Continue layering until you have used all the ingredients.

4   Sift the cocoa over the top and refrigerate for at least 2–3 hours before serving.

# Matt Moran and Andrew Honeysett's chocolate tart

Round three of the MasterChef grand finale was a pressure test. Matt Moran carried in a chocolate tasting plate, one of his signature dishes – not the full version served at ARIA, but one that had been simplified so Poh and Julie would at least stand a chance of completing the challenge within their allotted two and a half hours. The highly technical dish nevertheless involved about nine different processes, all of which included some form of chocolate. Four million Australians were watching as the two finalists got started.

Both Julie and Poh plated up in time and hugged each other as they waited for the judges' verdict. George gave Poh 7 points, while Gary, Matt and Curtis gave her 8 out of 10. All four judges gave Julie 9 out of 10, making her Australia's first MasterChef. Confetti rained down and the other members of the Top Twenty cheered as Julie was reunited with her family.

Serves 6–8
Preparation time: 2 hours
Cooking time: about 35 mins

**Chocolate sorbet**
150 g caster sugar
500 g Valrhona chocolate or
 an equivalent dark chocolate,
 chopped

**Chocolate pastry**
320 g plain flour
60 g dark cocoa powder
160 g caster sugar
160 g cold unsalted butter, diced
2 eggs

**Chocolate tart mixture**
210 g Valrhona chocolate or
 an equivalent dark chocolate,
 chopped
60 g milk chocolate, chopped
60 g unsalted butter, diced
315 ml cream
3 eggs
2 egg yolks

**Chocolate sauce**
60 g dark cocoa powder
120 g caster sugar
25 g butter, diced

**Chocolate icing**
(chocolate glaze)
300 g dark chocolate, chopped
240 ml cream

**Chocolate pipe**
250 g dark chocolate

**Chocolate macarons**
240 g icing sugar
125 g almond meal
25 g dark cocoa powder
100 g eggwhites (see note)

**To serve**
6 macarons, crumbled
250 ml double-thick cream

Method

1   To make the chocolate sorbet, combine the sugar and 800 ml water in a saucepan. Stir over medium-low heat until dissolved, then bring to the boil. Place the chocolate in a bowl and pour the syrup over. Stir until melted, then strain through a sieve. Cover the surface with cling film to avoid a skin forming, then place in the freezer until chilled. Place in the bowl of an ice-cream machine and churn for 5–10 mins or according to the manufacturer's instructions. Transfer to a container and place in the freezer until ready to use.

2   To make the chocolate pastry, preheat the oven to 180°C (160°C fan-forced). Place the flour, cocoa, sugar, butter and a pinch of salt in the bowl of a food processor and process until it resembles fine breadcrumbs. Add the eggs and process until dough just starts to come together. Turn on to a lightly floured surface and gently knead until just smooth. Flatten into a disc shape, cover with cling film, then place in the fridge for 30 mins to rest.

3   Roll out the pastry to a 15 x 40 cm rectangle, about 3 mm thick. Line the base and sides of a shallow 10 x 34 cm loose-based tart tin with the pastry, and trim any excess. Place in the fridge for 15 mins to rest. Line the pastry with baking paper and fill with baking weights or rice. Bake for 10 mins. Remove the paper and weights and bake for a further 5–10 mins or until firm to touch.

4   To make the chocolate sauce, combine the cocoa and sugar with 200 ml water in a saucepan. Stir over medium-low heat until the sugar dissolves, then bring to the boil. Stir in butter until melted, then strain through a fine sieve placed over a bowl.

5   To make the chocolate icing, place the chocolate in a bowl. Bring the cream to the boil in a saucepan, then pour over the chocolate. Stir until melted and smooth, then stir in the chocolate sauce.

6   To make the chocolate tart, preheat the oven to 160°C (140° fan-forced). Place the chocolate and butter in a bowl. Place cream in a saucepan and bring to boil. Pour the cream over the chocolate and butter and stir until smooth. Stir in the eggs and yolks. Fill the tart shell with chocolate mixture. Place remaining tart mixture into the fridge until mousse-like. Bake the tart for 25 mins or until cooked. The tart should have a slight wobble in the centre when it is ready. If it is not done, place it back into the oven for a further 5 mins. Cool the tart to room temperature, then ice with the chocolate icing. Reserve ⅓ cup of icing for presentation. Place the tart in the fridge until firm. Remove from the tart tin. Cut the tart into 7 rectangles, about 3–3.5 cm wide.

# Matt Moran and Andrew Honeysett's chocolate tart

7   To make the chocolate pipe, place 200 g of the chocolate in a bowl over a saucepan of barely simmering water. Warm the chocolate to 55°C. Remove the bowl from the heat and add the remaining chocolate. Leave to cool to 26–27°C. Place the bowl into the oven for 5 seconds to slightly warm or until chocolate is 30–31°C. Pour a spoonful of the tempered chocolate over a 4 x 25 cm sheet of acetate. Spread out with a palette knife and stand to partially set for 3–4 mins. Roll the sheet to fit and place inside the tube. Leave for about 1 hour, to set. Remove from the tube and peel away the acetate.

8   To make the chocolate macarons, preheat the oven to 150°C (130° fan-forced). Line a baking tray with non-stick baking paper. Sieve the sugar, almond meal and cocoa into a bowl. Beat the eggwhites until stiff peaks form, then slowly add the dry ingredients. Using a clean scraper, gently fold through. Transfer to a piping bag fitted with a plain nozzle, and pipe 4 mm rounds of mixture onto the prepared tray. Stand for 20–30 mins or until a skin has formed over the macarons. Bake for 6–8 mins or until set.

9   To make the macaron crumbs, preheat the oven to 150°C (130°C fan-forced) and line a baking tray with non-stick baking paper. Crumble 6 macarons to sand-like consistency onto the prepared tray. Bake for 10 mins or until dry. Cool.

10  To plate the dessert, first spread a little chocolate icing clockwise around half the plate. Place a slice of chocolate tart on top of the icing. Spread the base of a macaron with a small amount of the set tart filling. Place on the plate and top with a teaspoon quenelle of sorbet. Next place a small dot of the set tart filling on the plate and top with a spoonful of macaron crumbs. Place a teaspoon quenelle of double-thick cream on the crumbs. Finally, top the tart with a little spoon of set tart filling, then top with the chocolate pipe. (The tart filling will secure the chocolate pipe.)

Note A standard 59 g egg yields about 35 g of eggwhite. The best idea is to lightly whisk the eggwhites (this makes it easier to take some out if necessary), then weigh them to get the exact amount.

# Glossaries

Ingredients | Terms | Equipment

# Glossary of ingredients

00 flour This is an Italian description for plain flour. The 00 refers to how finely the flour is ground, 00 being the finest (other grades being 0 or 1). It does not necessarily refer to the protein content.

agar agar A thickening and setting agent similar to gelatine. It is derived from seaweed and is therefore a vegetarian alternative to gelatine.

allspice This is a berry which is used in a dried and ground form. It is not a blend of spices, though the flavour is like a combination of nutmeg, cinnamon and cloves.

bakers' grade plain flour This flour has a high protein (gluten) content, contributing to good structure in bread.

black vinegar A Chinese vinegar, made from black glutinous rice. Available from Asian food shops.

bottarga Dried grey mullet roe.

bouquet garni A traditional French herb combination of bay leaves, thyme sprigs and parsley stalks. These are tied together with kitchen string, or wrapped in muslin, and added to any stew-type dish that is slow-cooked for a good length of time. The string or muslin makes for easy retrieval and is always discarded after cooking.

century eggs Duck, chicken or quail eggs that have been preserved. Sometimes known as hundred-year eggs or thousand-year eggs. They are available from Asian food shops.

cep mushrooms Also known as porcini. A small, fleshy mushroom, often used in dried form.

Chinese rice wine See shaoxing wine

cornichons Tiny pickled cucumbers, smaller than a gherkin.

crème fraîche A cream product similar to sour cream, but richer and higher in fat. It has a culture added to it that gives it a characteristic tangy flavour.

dark cocoa Also known as Dutch cocoa, this is darker in colour than regular cocoa powder and preferred for use as a garnish for desserts.

edible metallic dust Available from cake-decorating suppliers, edible metallic dust comes in gold, silver and a huge range of other colours.

hail sugar A coarse white sugar used to decorate cakes and biscuits, available from cake-decorating suppliers.

inverted sugar A sucrose-based syrup available from cake-decorating or candy-making supply shops.

Jivara chocolate Jivara is a milk chocolate with 40% cocoa content and added malt, made by French manufacturer Valrhona and sold at specialty or gourmet food stores or online. If you can't find it, a good-quality dark chocolate with a high cocoa content is the next best thing.

king brown mushrooms Also known as king trumpet mushrooms, they are related to the oyster mushroom. They have a very wide stem, and the cap is small – not much wider than the stem. They are not widely available, but ask your greengrocer, who should be able to source them.

leaf gelatine Gelatine comes in two forms, leaf and powdered. Leaf is favoured by chefs as it gives a lovely clear finish. The 'leaf' is actually a sheet, and is softened in water before being added to the other ingredients. Available from specialty food shops.

liposoluble food colour Food colouring that blends easily into oil-based substances such as chocolate or buttercream. It is available from cake-decorating suppliers.

micro-herbs Young shoots of herbs or salad greens, which usually have just the first two leaves. Used to garnish. These are available growing in punnets from good greengrocers. Just use scissors to snip off at ground level.

morel A type of mushroom with a high, elongated cap and a honeycomb texture on the outside. Often used in dried form.

pectin nh An ingredient used in patisserie to give a glossy appearance and desirable texture to coatings and mixtures. Available from cake-decorating suppliers.

piquillo pepper A Spanish chilli. They are short and wide with a pointed end (piquillo means 'little beak'). They are often roasted and stuffed.

porcini mushrooms See cep mushrooms

salted duck eggs Duck eggs preserved in brine or a salted clay mixture, available from Asian food shops.

shaoxing wine/Chinese rice wine A Chinese wine fermented from rice that is drunk as a beverage and used in cooking, especially for marinating meats. Available from Asian food shops.

shiitake mushrooms A mushroom used in Asian cookery, particularly Chinese and Japanese. They are widely available fresh or dried.

tofu Soy bean curd. Firm tofu is easily chopped and tossed through stir-fries; silken tofu is fragile but has a very smooth texture.

tonka beans These beans are from South America, and are used in a similar way to vanilla beans, to impart fragrance and flavour to sweet dishes. They should be used sparingly as they can cause health problems.

veal glace/veal glaze/veal jus Veal stock that has been reduced to intensify its flavour. You can buy it in a jar from a good delicatessen or specialty shop.

verjuice A vinegar-type ingredient, made by pressing unfermented grapes. It is milder than vinegar or lemon juice, but is used in much the same way in dressings and sauces.

vialone nano A round, short-grain rice grown in Veneto, Italy. The round grains are able to soak up twice their weight in liquid, making it the perfect rice for risotto.

white balsamic Not a true balsamic vinegar, though it has a similar flavour. It is good to use when you don't want the colour of a dish affected by dark balsamic vinegar.

# Glossary of terms

amuse-bouche A tiny one- or two-bite portion of food, brought to the table before a meal, designed to stimulate the appetite and interest in the courses to follow. Literally, 'amuse mouth'.

aromatics Sometimes referred to as 'aromats', these ingredients infuse a dish with subtle base flavours. Bay leaves, thyme and peppercorns are examples, as are onion, carrots and celery.

blind bake To line an unbaked pastry shell with baking paper, and fill with pastry weights or dried beans. The pastry is partially cooked, then the paper and weights are removed before the cooking is finished. This ensures a dry base, and the weights prevent the base from puffing up during cooking.

blanch To immerse an ingredient in boiling water briefly to just par-cook. It is then often plunged into iced water to stop the cooking process. Blanching helps green vegetables retain their colour.

caramelise To cook sugar until it melts and becomes golden brown in colour. Caramelisation occurs in many foods, including meat and vegetables, because of naturally occurring sugars present. Caramelisation is generally desirable because it indicates good flavour.

deglaze To add a liquid to a pan – for instance, to dislodge caramelised pan juices after frying meat.

docking To prick pastry with a fork or small knife, to prevent air pockets forming during cooking.

egg wash Lightly beaten egg, sometimes mixed with water or milk, used to brush uncooked baked goods to create a glaze when cooked.

emulsion A mixture that is evenly mixed, and stays that way on standing. (Mayonnaise is an example: it is an emulsion of oil and egg yolks.) If not mixed properly, the mixture will curdle and/or separate.

foaming butter Melting butter in a pan over high heat until it foams.

julienne To cut vegetables such as carrots into thin 'matchsticks'.

pin bone To remove tiny bones in fish, usually with specially designed tweezers.

quenelle Soft food (such as a puree, cream or mousse-like mixture, either savoury or sweet), formed into a neat oval shape by scooping and moulding using two spoons.

sofrito A flavoursome sautéed base mixture to which other ingredients are added. In Spain, a sofrito is usually onion, garlic and tomatoes cooked down in olive oil, to begin a paella.

sous vide French for 'under vacuum'. It means that food is sealed in plastic from which all the oxygen has been expelled, and then cooked at a low temperature, which preserves the colour and texture of the food and, in the case of meat, contributes to a very tender product.

sweat To cook food in a little butter or oil over low heat until soft.

temper Tempering chocolate is heating it and then cooling it again to achieve a smooth, glossy finish and a crisp snap. Tempered chocolate is used for coating other ingredients, for moulding and for dipping.

# Glossary of equipment

cake ring A metal ring with no base, used to assemble desserts and cakes, available from kitchenware shops.

chinois A fine-meshed conical sieve. Liquid runs out more quickly from a chinois than a round-bottomed sieve.

croquembouche cone A tall metal cone used to construct a croquembouche. They can be hired from kitchenware shops. A clean plastic traffic cone is a DIY alternative.

dariole mould A small, cylindrical mould used to shape desserts for attractive presentation. Made from stainless steel, aluminium and sometimes plastic.

drum sieve A wide, fine-meshed, flat-bottomed sieve, usually used to press cooked food through, to make a finely textured puree.

loose-based tart tin These come in various sizes and shapes, and usually have fluted sides. They are normally used for open tarts. The loose base sits inside, making it easy to lift the finished tart from the tin.

mandolin An implement used to cut vegetables evenly. The blade is usually adjustable so you can cut to your desired thickness with uniform results.

mortar and pestle A bowl (mortar) and stick (pestle) made from heavy stone or ceramic material, used for grinding and pounding ingredients such as spices. A food processor or spice grinder may be used instead.

paring knife A small knife used to peel and trim vegetables and fruit.

pizza stone A flat piece of (usually) terracotta, which you place into a cold oven and then heat to a high temperature. The uncooked pizza is placed directly onto the stone, which distributes heat evenly and absorbs moisture from the base, giving a crisp result. A terracotta tile may be used, but it must be unglazed.

thermometers Different types of thermometers perform different tasks in the kitchen.

– A sugar thermometer tells you when a sugar syrup reaches different stages. Used when making confectionery.

– A thermometer that registers lower temperatures is needed for tempering chocolate.

– A deep-frying thermometer is used to check the heat of oil for deep-frying. As these thermometers and sugar thermometers register high temperatures, they are interchangeable.

– An oven thermometer sits in the oven and is used to ensure the correct temperature. Have your oven calibrated if you think it is out by a significant amount.

– A meat thermometer is inserted into meat to check its internal temperature during roasting.

silicone paper Paper treated with a silicone finish to make it non-stick. Used to line cake tins and baking trays.

spray guns Spray guns are sold at hardware stores. If you buy one for your kitchen, use it only for food.

vacuum There is now a domestic version of the vacuum-packing machine on the market that you can use for sous vide cooking. They are available from large department stores and electrical retailers.

# Contributing chefs

Martin Boetz – www.longrain.com

Martin Boetz is executive chef at Longrain Sydney and Longrain Melbourne. He is considered one of Australia's leading talents in contemporary Thai-style Asian cooking, having worked with mentor David Thompson at Darley Street Thai and Sailors Thai. His book, *Longrain: Modern Thai Food*, is published by Hardie Grant Books and is available internationally.

Donovan Cooke

Donovan Cooke is chef de cuisine at the Derby Restaurant & Bar at the Happy Valley Clubhouse at The Hong Kong Jockey Club. He was named Chef of the Year by *The Age Good Food Guide* in 2003/2004 after opening the now legendary Melbourne restaurants est est est and Ondine, and was made Honorary Commandeur of La Commanderie des Cordons Bleus de France for his outstanding culinary achievements in 2005. His cookbook, *Marriages*, is published by New Holland.

Pete Evans – www.hugos.com.au

Pete Evans is the managing director of the Hugos Group: Hugos Bar Pizza and Hugos Lounge Kings Cross, Hugos Manly and the Pantry, Melbourne. He is the author of *Fish*, *My Table*, and his latest book, *My Grill: Food for the Barbecue*, published by Murdoch.

Manu Feildel – www.letoilerestaurant.com.au

Formerly head chef at Bilson's Restaurant, Manu Feildel is now chef de cuisine at his own restaurant, Manu at L'étoile, in Paddington, Sydney. He regularly appears on television shows including *Ready Steady Cook* and *9am with David & Kim*.

Guy Grossi – www.grossi.com.au

Guy Grossi is owner and executive chef at Melbourne's Grossi Florentino and its sister restaurant, Mirka at Tolarno Hotel, as well as the recently established Grossi Trattoria, Bangkok. He has written two books: *Guy Grossi: My Italian Heart* and *Grossi Florentino: Secrets & Recipes*, published by Penguin Australia.

Alex Herbert – www.birdcowfish.com.au

Alex Herbert began her apprenticeship at Berowra Waters Inn, under the direction of Gay Bilson and Janni Kyritsis. Since 2006 she has been co-owner and head chef at Bird Cow Fish in Sydney's Surry Hills, where she holds regular Regional Wine and Produce dinners and Food Writer dinners. The team from Bird Cow Fish can also be found serving breakfast at Eveleigh Market in Redfern every Saturday morning.

## Matt Moran and Andrew Honeysett – www.ariarestaurant.com

Matt Moran is co-owner and chef at ARIA Restaurant in Sydney and the recently opened ARIA Brisbane. He was resident top chef on Channel 9's reality cooking show *The Chopping Block* and is the author of two cookbooks, *Matt Moran* and *When I Get Home*. Matt works in collaboration with Andrew Honeysett, ARIA's pastry chef, to create and refine desserts such as the fabulous chocolate tart seen in the MasterChef finale.

## Ben O'Donoghue – www.benodonoghue.com

Chef and television presenter Ben O'Donoghue is best known in Australia as the man behind the acclaimed food and travel program, *Surfing the Menu*, but he has also worked as executive chef at prestigious London restaurants and published several cookbooks, including *Outdoor: Grill Your Way 'Round the World*, *Surfing the Menu*, *Surfing the Menu Again* and *The Best*.

## Adrian Richardson – www.lalunabistro.com.au

Adrian Richardson is owner and executive chef at La Luna in North Carlton, specialising in 'modern Mediterranean'. Adrian has worked in some of Melbourne's best restaurants, including Toofey's with Michael Bacash, and O'Connell's with Greg Malouf. He is the author of *Meat*, published by Hardie Grant Books, and has made numerous television appearances on shows including *Boys Weekend*, *9am with David & Kim* and *Ready Steady Cook*.

## Frank Shek – www.chinadoll.com.au

Frank Shek is executive chef at China Doll on Sydney's historic Finger Wharf at Woolloomooloo, and specialises in modern Asian dishes from Japan, Hong Kong, China and South-East Asia.

## Emmanuel Stroobant – www.emmanuelstroobant.com

Expatriate Belgian Emmanuel Stroobant and his partner Edina Hong moved to Singapore in 1999 and opened Saint Pierre the following year. They now run a series of restaurants. He has written two cookbooks: *Cuisine Unplugged* and *Vine Dining – White*, both published by Marshall Cavendish. Emmanuel has also starred in his own TV series, *Chef in Black*.

## Adriano Zumbo – adrianozumbo.com

Pastry chef Adriano Zumbo's production kitchen in Sydney's Rozelle supplies his two existing retail outlets, the Artisan Patisserie and Café Chocolat. Plans are in place for a third bakery-style cafe. Adriano and his creations have featured in *Gourmet Traveller*, *Vogue Entertainment and Travel*, *Good Living*, *The Sydney Magazine* and *Time Out*, and he has just started work on a book, to be released in 2010.

# Photography

All on-set photography by Stuart Bryce.

Food photography by Alan Richardson and styling by Trish Heagerty, except where otherwise noted.

Crispy chips, page 39; Classic roast potatoes, page 40; Pomme puree, page 43; Julie's steak with tarragon salt, page 175; and Lemon curd, page 203: styling by Kristen Wilson.

Brent's Italian vegetables, page 49: photograph by Brent Parker Jones, styling by Briony Bennett and Lee Blaylock.

Nic's aglio e olio, page 51: photograph by Brent Parker Jones, styling by Briony Bennett and Lee Blaylock.

Martin Boetz's eggnets, page 68: photograph by Jeremy Simons of Vivid Productions, supplied by Longrain (www.longrain.com).

Sam's pan-roasted chicken with potato and zucchini rosti, page 86: photograph by Brent Parker Jones, styling by Briony Bennett and Lee Blaylock.

Brent's Top Fifty salt and pepper squid, page 141: photograph by Brent Parker Jones, styling by Briony Bennett and Lee Blaylock.

Guy Grossi's insalata di arrigosta con insalata ruselle, page 143: photograph by Adrian Lander, taken from *Grossi Florentino: Secrets & Recipes* by Guy Grossi and Jan McGuinness, published in Lantern by Penguin Group Australia, Melbourne, 2007, page 172. Reproduced with permission of Penguin Group (Australia).

Aaron's beef pithivier, page 176: photograph by Greg Elms, styling by Aaron Thomas.

Brent's braised rabbit in a capsicum, tomato and fennel sauce, page 178: photograph by Brent Parker Jones, styling by Briony Bennett and Lee Blaylock.

Ben O'Donoghue's seared kangaroo with creamed corn, page 181: photograph by Andre Martin, styling by Trish Heagerty.

Matt Moran's warm pear tart, page 213: photograph by Murray Fredericks, supplied by ARIA Restaurant.

Linda's blueberry and violet rice pudding, page 218: photograph by Greg Elms, styling by Linda Kowalski.

ARIA chocolate tart by Matt Moran and Andrew Honeysett, page 243: photograph by Murray Fredericks, supplied by ARIA Restaurant.

# Acknowledgements

A huge thankyou to all the MasterChef Top Twenty contestants for contributing the recipes and stories that make up this book: Chris Badenoch, Josh Catalano, Nic Ciampa, Sam Ciaravolo, Michelle Darlington, Trevor Forster, Julie Goodwin, Julia Jenkins, Linda Kowalski, Melissa Lutton, Sandra Moreno, Tom Mosby, Geni Papacostas, Brent Parker Jones, Lucas Parsons, Kate Rodrigues, Justine Schofield, Aaron Thomas, André Ursini and Poh Ling Yeow.

Thanks also to the chefs who generously contributed their recipes, took the time to field queries, supplied images, organised photoshoots, let our photographers loose in their restaurants, and cooked up some beautiful dishes for the camera: Martin Boetz, Donovan Cooke, Pete Evans, Manu Feildel, Guy Grossi, Alex Herbert, Andrew Honeysett, Matt Moran, Ben O'Donoghue, Adrian Richardson, Frank Shek, Emmanuel Stroobant and Adriano Zumbo.

Massive and heartfelt gratitude to everyone who worked so hard to get this book off to print in an impossibly short time: Tracy Rutherford, Trish Heagerty, Kellie Thomas, Nick Eade, Angela Muscat, Samantha Joel, Kirrily La Rosa, Kristen Wilson and Tricia Dearborn. Special thanks to Alan Richardson and Chloe Stevens for giving up their front room, kitchen, back garden and weekends for more than a month; and to Ingo Voss for the long days and unfailing good humour under pressure.

For the fantastic live-action shots, thanks to Stuart Bryce, and for the gorgeous food photography, thanks to Alan Richardson, Brent Parker Jones, Greg Elms and Andre Martin.

For help in sourcing images and organising photoshoots, thanks to: the staff at Bird Cow Fish, China Doll, Hugos Kings Cross, L'etoile and Adriano Zumbo's Café Chocolat; Karen Evans and Megan Lowe at ARIA Restaurant; Elizabeth Grossi at Grossi Florentino; Chelsia Chung of The Hong Kong Jockey Club; Lynda at La Luna Bistro; Kathy at Longrain; Edina Hong and Gene Mok of Saint Pierre; Justine May at Chef's Ink; Lisa Sullivan at Forum5; Lindy Thompson of Lindy Thompson PR; Cathy Baker at Profile Talent Management; Melissa Leong; Julie Pinkham at Hardie Grant; and Peg McColl and Kate McCormack at Penguin.

For arranging props and equipment, thanks to MaryAnne Fesq at Villeroy & Boch and everyone at To Health By Choice. Special thanks to Meredith Conolly at Sheldon & Hammond.

To Nikki Christer, Elizabeth Cowell, Nikla Martin and everyone at Random House Australia, thanks for the incredible effort and hard work it took to bring this project together.

Finally, a big thankyou to everyone at FremantleMedia Australia, especially Prue Mann, Kate Nichols, Candi Bloxham, Victoria Carr, Nellie Connors, Olivia Arnold and Ben Liebmann.

Equipment supplied by:

# Index

# Index

# Index

# Index